Eng

D1796141

Stage to Nowhere

Stage to Nowhere

William Hirst

NELSON

Thomas Nelson and Sons Ltd
Nelson House Mayfield Road
Walton-on-Thames Surrey KT12 5PL
P.O. Box 18123 Nairobi Kenya
116-D JTC Factory Building
Lorong 3 Geylang Square Singapore 1438

Thomas Nelson Australia Pty Ltd
19–39 Jeffcott Street West Melbourne Victoria 3003

Nelson Canada Ltd
81 Curlew Drive Don Mills Ontario M3A 2R1

Thomas Nelson (Hong Kong) Ltd
Watson Estate Block A 13 Floor
Watson Road Causeway Bay Hong Kong

Thomas Nelson (Nigeria) Ltd
8 Ilupeju Bypass PMB 21303 Ikeja Lagos

Cover design by Mandy Prout

Printed and bound in Hong Kong

One

It was about mid-morning when Sam rode alone out of the little mining town of Narrow Bend. The sun, blazing from the West Texas sky, did nothing to ease the worst sore head he had ever had.

'Whisky!' he groaned. 'If only I hadn't drunk all that whisky—I should never touch that tonsil-paint—beer's always been all right for me, so why . . . ?'

His excuse had been that because it was his last night in town, he should drink a lot of goodbyes, but he was mighty sorry for it now.

And Straw wasn't helping any. Straw was his horse, and Sam was proud of her. She was full of spirit, and on this morning wanting to be off stretching her legs down that empty trail. She didn't, like Sam, have a bad head and a wish just to go quietly along.

Sam groaned for the umpteenth time. Never again! No more whisky from now on. Not one more drop. He allowed Straw to get from a walk into a trot, but in no time at all she had sneaked into a canter.

'Hold on there, Straw,' grumbled Sam. 'Ain't you got no feeling for me at all?'

Although the trail stretched empty before him, Sam still kept a good look-out all round. These were badlands and law didn't stretch far outside a town's limits. Out here you were on your own.

The view was marvellous, from the tumbling foothills on his right rising around the high white peaks of the Snake Mountains, to the rock-strewn sandy-lands stretching into the shimmering distance on his left.

But Sam was in no mood for admiring views. Besides the ache in his head, he had an ache in his pocket. A hundred and ten dollars he had been winning in that game of Faro last night. A hundred and ten dollars! And how much had he left? He knew without taking it out and counting it.

Eighteen dollars! After all the whisky and wild betting, just eighteen dollars left. He should have had more sense. It was worse than bunkhouse gambling. Still, why worry, at least it was eighteen dollars—it could have been nothing.

Sam slowed Straw to her usual trot and tried, in vain, to forget his head. The sun got higher and hotter until, a couple of hours later, Sam could stand it no more.

By that time it seemed to Sam that the sun had come right down to about two feet above his Stetson, and was doing its best to melt him into the ground. He decided to stop and make camp. And maybe rest a while in the shade of a rock.

He chose a big rock which cast a cool shadow, but at the same time gave him a good view of the foothills. That was where the trouble would come from—if there was any trouble around.

He was in no hurry, but he left Straw saddled and ground-hitched. In these parts you never knew when a quick getaway was needed. Straw was all right, she wouldn't wander—and anyway he was keeping a close eye on her, wasn't he?

He ate a little pan-baked biscuit, then rolled a cigarette and smoked it sitting on the ground and leaning back against the warm rock. He pushed his hat forward to shade his eyes as he looked across at the foothills that waved and danced in the heat.

He stubbed out the butt in the sand and made himself more comfortable. His elbows were in the soft sand, his fingers laced across just above his gun-belt, his hat was forward almost touching his nose. Very comfortable—it made his head feel a lot better just resting like this. He brushed off a few flies then closed his eyes against the glare.

Just a few minutes. Then he'd make a move. Say five minutes, then he'd be on his way again. Just five minutes . . .

He awoke with a feeling that something was wrong. He also felt guilty about having dozed off. Only a fool would sleep in broad daylight out in the open in country like this.

Yet he could not shake off his sleep. His head still ached and his eyes were heavy and dull. He seemed to be in a daze. That whisky last night and now the hot sun . . .

Then it came again—the noise that had wakened him— a loud laugh followed by more laughing—almost giggles. He pushed up his hat and forced his eyes open against the glare.

Four Indians sat on their ponies and laughed as they looked down at him.

He could see why they were laughing. An arrow was sticking in the sand between his boots. The Indian who had fired it was fitting another arrow to his bow, but even as he did so, one of the others fired. His arrow struck the sand within an inch of Sam's wrist.

He snatched his hand away and they all laughed again. It was a game of who could get nearest and who would care if you got too near?

The third Indian was just watching. He was carrying an old Sharps rifle.

Before another arrow could be fired, the fourth Indian decided it was his turn for some fun. He was a thin, lanky youth, unarmed, but with painted cheeks and smelling strongly of bear grease. He slid off his pony and before

7

Sam was really awake to what was happening, he had run across to Straw.

As Indians mount their horses from the right, this one had to go to the side of Straw away from Sam. The next moment the Indian was up in Straw's saddle and turning to shout to the others. At the same time he was pulling hard on the reins with one hand and reaching for the Winchester in the saddle scabbard with the other.

Straw was not used to such rough handling – or the smell of bear grease – and she reared sharply. The Indian hung on. It was then made very clear that this Indian had a very direct way of dealing with high-spirited horses. He smashed his clenched fist hard down on Straw's head between her ears. Straw neighed shrilly and shook her head. Again she reared and once more the Indian raised his fist.

The hurt sound of Straw's neigh got through Sam's after-sleep haze and when he looked up and saw that fist raised again, he was overcome with rage.

He threw himself forward on to his knees in the sand. At the same time he drew his gun with a speed fed by his anger and shot at the Indian on Straw's back.

He aimed high so that he would not hit Straw as she reared and plunged. The Indian shouted in pain and clapped his hand to his shoulder. His body bowed forward in his effort to keep his balance.

Without waiting to see what effect his shot had, Sam whirled round on the other Indians who were raising their bows. He kept his trigger pressed and fanned off four shots so fast that they almost sounded like one.

These shots, wildly fired, all missed the Indians, but the sudden blast of them set two of the ponies rearing. One Indian slid sideways to the ground and began jerking savagely at the single rein. Another dropped his bow as he fought for control of his pony which was lashing the air with its unshod hooves.

8

The third Indian was the one with the old Sharps rifle and his horse had missed the full force of the blast. He was able to bring his gun to bear on Sam and it seemed that in a matter of a couple of seconds all would be over for Sam.

At that moment the Indian on Straw's back fell out of the saddle and rolled against the legs of the third Indian's horse. This made the animal rear in fright and the Sharps went off sending its bullet climbing high into the air.

For a few moments all was confusion as the wounded Indian rolled to and fro on the ground, trying to get to his feet and making it impossible for the other Indians to control their mounts.

This was time enough for Sam to scramble forward on to his feet, thrust his gun back into his holster and throw himself into the saddle.

'Come on, Straw!' he yelled.

Straw needed no urging and was in full gallop from a standing start. Sam urged her on still faster, hoping that if he got a good lead the Indians would not take up the chase, yet knowing they would.

Straw tore across the rough ground towards the foothills. As the Indians had been on the trail and Straw was racing away from them, Sam could see that they could do nothing but head further and further away from the trail in the direction of the foothills.

He looked over his shoulder and saw that three of the Indians were already chasing along behind him on their fleet Indian ponies. No heavy saddles to weigh them down, thought Sam.

Already they were gaining on him and he could hear their wild cries of excitement and threat.

Yet in the midst of all this, the next thought that went through his mind was one of regret about his hat that had fallen off in his wild scramble.

Pity about that hat. Had that hat for three years—since

I was seventeen. Then the shrill cries from behind reminded him that he might lose his hair as well as his hat if he couldn't outrun them.

The Indian must have reloaded the single-shot Old Reliable, for the heavy report of the Sharps came to him. He was not afraid of being hit by a bullet fired from horseback. That Indian couldn't aim from the back of a wildly-galloping pony. Of course it was always possible for an unlucky bullet to hit Straw.

He could fire back with his Winchester, but he knew he had only a few rounds left in it. He must buy some if he got out of this alive. He urged Straw on faster over the rough ground, hoping that she would not put one of her hooves in a gopher hole because then . . .

By this time the trail was far behind, and there was no chance of getting back to it. If he tried that they would easily cut him off. There was only one way left to him, and that was straight on towards the foothills. One good thing was that Straw was really getting into her stride, and the Indians were no longer gaining ground.

Sam took a quick look all round, but as far as he could see the landscape was empty. The only moving things were the three Indians whooping and lashing their ponies behind him. There was no help at all for him.

Two

Sam's mind whirled round the problem. He could stop and lie in wait for them. By the time they got to him he could be behind some big boulder with a chance of picking them off with his Winchester.

No, no good. That was no way to do it. They'd just take

10

cover, pin him down there and attack from three sides—or wait till dark ...

It looked like the only thing he could do was to outrun them. He set Straw's head for the beginning of the foothills which were then not far away. Looking back again he saw that the three were well spread in a line behind him. The last was lagging far behind, but the nearest one was well ahead of the others.

He must have a better pony or a stronger right arm, thought Sam.

The cries had died away as though the Indians realised that it was not going to be a quick victory, but a hard slog for them to catch this white-eyes again.

The first slopes of the barren foothills slowed Straw so that the nearest Indian drew within easy arrow shot. But when the Indian hit the slopes then Sam began to widen the gap between them.

On they went, up and up a long slope, then along a ridge, then up again, through a short canyon, up rock-covered hills and round great rocks.

Straw topped a rise and began to blow. Sam stopped to look round. The two slower Indians were a long way back, but the other one, the leader, was still keeping up a good pace. His pony was striding well with its head still up.

Sam decided to find a good spot and waylay the leader. If he could get him, there was a good chance that the other two would give up. He rode along another ridge looking for a good place for an ambush. The trail to Bear Cross was long out of sight and all around were the rolling foothills. He rode up another slope and there he came to the ideal place.

There was a short and fairly steep hill, with a couple of big rocks at the top. He could get Straw behind the rocks and then wait. The Indian would slow down a lot on the

11

hill and that would give Sam a chance for a sure shot with his Winchester.

He urged Straw on faster up the hill. Every second counted. Once at the top he swung out of the saddle, grabbed the Winchester and smacked Straw's haunches to send her off behind the rock where she'd be safe. It took only seconds to scramble up the rock and lie on top of it with a clear view of the ground below him.

He slid his rifle forward, his cheek resting against the worn stock. He waited. Any second now the Indian would burst into view and come racing—as hard as a spent pony could race—up the slope and Sam would be ready for him.

The seconds passed. There was silence apart from the buzzing of a few insects and the faint jangle of Straw's bit. More seconds passed. The glaring heat brought little lights to dance before his eyes.

Then he was there. The Indian appeared at the bottom of the slope, but instead of charging up, he reined in his pony and stopped. He sat there, half in the shadow of a rock and he looked up the slope. Sam could see, even at that distance, that the pony was blown.

He tightened his grip on his rifle. What was happening? Was the Indian waiting for the others to catch up? It seemed not, for the Indian was looking forwards, not backwards as though waiting for his companions. He was looking straight at the rock where Sam was waiting, his keen eyes searched for a sign, for the slightest movement.

Maybe this ground had been used for ambush in the past, thought Sam. The Indian was wary. He did not move. His pony waved its head and snorted.

Sam slowly moved his rifle so that the sights were centred on the Indian. He aimed at the Indian's half-shadowed chest. It would be a good shot if he hit him, but he knew he could do it. His finger tightened on the trigger. He held his breath.

12

Suddenly, as though sensing his danger, the Indian gave a quick wave of his hand towards the top of the slope. He wheeled his pony and vanished back the way he had come.

Sam let go his breath in a sigh. Sweat trickled down his face. He grinned at nothing in particular. He knew that deep down he was glad he didn't have to shoot the Indian. Yet if it had come to a fight he wouldn't have thought twice about it. He'd learned that in a land as tough as this, most of the time second thoughts were weak thoughts.

He wriggled off the top of the rock and, bending double, he zig-zagged his way round the other rocks. He was aiming for a high flat-topped rock standing taller than the rest. Once on top of that he would be able to see for miles around.

Gasping in the heat and with his head throbbing, he lay on top of the rough sandy rock and gazed back the way he had come on his hectic ride. Shading his eyes with his hands he took a long look into the distance.

He could not see the trail. He could not see far beyond the foothills. For minutes he stared until his eyes ached and smarted and watered, but he saw them. There were two spots of dust close together and then another, larger and nearer and far behind the other two. It was all right. They had given up and gone back. Gone, he supposed, to collect their wounded comrade—the horse-beater.

Sam walked slowly back to where Straw was still waiting patiently beside the big rock. He rode on letting her pick her way along the rock-littered hill while he wondered what to do.

Which way should he go now? He was miles from the trail. Better not go back—no sense in chancing more trouble with the Indians. He guessed he was not far from Snake Pass and where there was a pass there was bound to be a trail. He decided to keep going and head that way.

Soon he was travelling along a maze of ridges and shallow valleys with dry river-beds between the ridges. At times he was surprised to come across long patches of tall yellow grass growing out of the parched ground. He kept a sharp lookout for signs of other travellers, but for an hour nothing unusual met his sun-weary eyes.

Then he rode up the side of a ridge and was about to ride down the other when he stopped in amazement. There, down below and along a piece and stopped on a narrow sort of track, was a stage-coach.

Not only was *that* there—a full-sized stage-coach—but there were six horses hitched to it. Both doors on the stage were open, but there was no one in sight.

Sam quickly turned Straw back down the ridge, the way he had come. He slid from the saddle, took out his Winchester and crawled back to the top. Carefully, showing as little of himself as possible, he lay and looked down over the scene below.

He had not been dreaming. He was not seeing things because he had been too long in the sun without his hat. There was the stage-coach right enough. A stage and six horses, but, it seemed, nothing and no one else.

He lay and waited for several minutes, but nothing moved. He could see the name *Wells, Fargo Bear Cross Line* painted on the side of the coach above the door.

The six horses stood and waited. There was still no sign of anyone—no driver or passengers. Sam was as wary now as the Indian had been at the bottom of that slope back there. Was this some kind of trap? Was this coach some sort of bait for an ambush? But how could it be? And why? And certainly not for him. He hadn't known himself that he would come this way.

When a couple of slow minutes had passed he could wait no longer. He got up and began to walk down the hill towards the coach. As he got nearer the horses began to show interest. They turned their heads to look at him and
14

moved restlessly. The leaders strained against their collars, but the stage stayed still.

Sam went over to the open door and looked in. There were benches covered in a very worn red plush, but nothing else. The coach was empty—no people—no luggage—no bodies of shot passengers—no arrows stuck in the woodwork—no signs of a struggle—nothing. He closed the door.

He walked round the back of the stage to the other side. He closed the other door—for no good reason except that it was open.

There seemed nothing out of place, except the whole foolish thing. The whole coach was out of place. A big empty coach and six horses up in the foothills on a lonely track and maybe miles from the trail—for what?

It was a wonder the horses hadn't wandered on and maybe tipped the coach into a hole or broken a wheel against a rock or whatever sort of accidents stages have.

Then Sam saw, on the wheels, the brakes pressed tightly. Ah, that was it. The brakes were on and that was why the horses weren't pulling the stage around. That was why . . . but then, if the brake was on, then that meant the stage was driven here and left. Now why should anybody . . .

He put his foot on the hub of the front wheel and pulled himself up into the driver's seat. He grabbed a little rail with one hand, still holding his Winchester in the other.

This was the first time he had been up on a stage—it was pretty high. That was the brake handle—the reins were neatly fastened to it. Next to the driver would sit the guard. He would sit there and he would . . .

Then he saw the blood stains. They were on the seat and on the footboard—great brown drops and streaks. Even on the back of one of the horses were more splashes.

What was it all about? It seemed certain that the coach had been held up, but what had happened to everybody?

15

There must have been shooting with the guard wounded
—killed?—but where was he?

Suddenly he heard Straw whinny and saw her top the
ridge and start down towards him. He grinned. She never
did like being left by herself. He watched her till she
started nibbling grass that grew between the rocks.

He turned in the seat and looked back along the top of
the coach. There was a pigskin water-bag—about half full.
Didn't seem to be anything wrong up there. Nothing except the blood stains. Maybe the best thing for him to do
was. . .

'All right, don't move!' The man's voice came from
behind him. 'Throw your rifle over the side.'

Sam hesitated.

'Come on, or you're dead . . .'

Three

Sam pitched the rifle down—even in that surprised
moment trying to make it land on soft sand and not on
hard rock.

'Now put your hands up and turn round real slow.'

Sam put up his hands and slowly turned in the driving
seat towards the voice. He could see nothing except the
muzzle of a rifle jutting over a rock at the top of the ridge.
Just above the rifle was a hat. The rifle was sighted on
Sam and there was surely, he thought uneasily, a finger
curled round the trigger.

'Jump down!'

Sam jumped off the coach and landed with his arms still
held high.

'Now unbuckle your belt and drop it.'

Sam made only the slightest hesitation, but it was enough to cause the rifle to fire. A bullet ploughed the ground at his feet and the horses shifted nervously. The leaders reared a little, rattling their harness. From the corner of his eye, Sam saw Straw trot away round to the back of the coach.

He unbuckled his belt and let it drop, then he put up his hands again. This was a man to take no chances with.

The voice came again.

'Back up by the stage door.' Sam did this. 'Now put your hands down.'

Sam leaned back against the door with the sun hot on his face. He could see very clearly the light glinting on the rifle barrel.

What could he do now? Who was that feller up there? Sam shook his head slowly. This was not one of his good days. What had he got into now? What could he do to get out of it? This feller had the drop on him all right. What next? Maybe the stranger would get up and come down to him. That should start something. At least he could talk to the man about it—show him how wrong he was. Yeah, that was it. He'd have to come down.

But the stranger did not come down. Minutes passed and Sam stood and sweated with his back against the hot coach. The horses settled down to their patient waiting again. He could not see Straw, but he guessed that she had wandered off down the track.

What was the man waiting for—if he was still there. Was he still there? Sam could not see any glinting light any more.

He pushed himself off the coach. Nothing much—just straightening up. Not much more than easing his position, but the voice came again.

'Hold it! You try anything and I'll put a hole right through you before you take a step—or even half a step.'

I guess he would too, thought Sam. He relaxed again. His feet felt sore, his head ached and he was thirsty. What wouldn't he give for some beer right now.

At that moment there was the sound of hooves and four men came riding round the bend in the track. They were four dusty men on four hot and dusty horses that looked as though they had come a long way.

They stopped in front of Sam—not quite getting in the line of fire. Now what? Then Sam saw a badge on a flannel shirt and gave a sigh. He was all right. The law had arrived.

'Sheriff . . .' he began, but the sheriff was not paying him any attention. He was looking up the ridge slope where the man with the rifle was coming down. Sam was surprised to see that he was only a young fellow about his own age. Now he came down the slope carrying his rifle and grinning at the sheriff as though he was mighty pleased with the little job he had done.

'So you got one, Des,' said the sheriff. 'Well done, son. Have you talked to him?'

'Naw, sheriff, he was up on the stage when I rode up and he was so took up with what he was doing he never heard me. I figured a shot would bring you here and,' he looked down at Sam, 'it kept him quiet.'

'Sheriff . . .' said Sam again.

The sheriff ignored him.

'This is one of 'em all right,' he said. 'I can smell 'em a mile off. Now let's see what we can get out of him.'

One of the others, a square, rubbery-faced man wearing shabby clothes, a well-worn Stetson and two guns swung off his horse and walked across to Sam. He pushed his face close to Sam's and glared at him.

'Where's the rest of 'em?' he asked in a quiet voice as though he was asking the way to the nearest town.

Sam lifted both hands, palms forward.

18

'Now listen, this has nothing to do with me. I . . .'

He stopped as the square man drew one of his guns.

'Wait a minute, Gordon,' said the sheriff. 'We'll hear him out if he don't take too long about it.'

Sam told his story fast and they all listened in silence. While he was talking, two more men rode up to join the group. These were more of the posse.

When Sam had finished, the sheriff stared at him with narrowed eyes.

'Don't believe you,' he said. 'Now, tell us, where are the others?'

Gordon pressed his gun against Sam's chest.

'Where are they?' he asked. 'Which way? Have they tried to get through the pass, or do they mean to stay this side of the mountain? Where are they going to hole up?'

'This is crazy,' said Sam. 'I don't know anything about all this. I told you, I came along just a few minutes before you did. I had nothing to do with any of this. Now do I look like one of them—whoever they are you're chasing?'

The sheriff rubbed his bristly chin and nodded.

'Yeah, I reckon you could—easily. I guess you can't go by looks too much. I've put a lot of honest-looking fellers in jail for all sorts of things.'

Gordon jabbed his gun again.

'Come on, spit it out!'

'Look, I don't know. I've told you what happened,' shouted Sam.

Gordon spoke to the sheriff without taking his eyes off Sam's face.

'What d'you think, sheriff? Shot while trying to escape?'

The sheriff was silent. This is a dream, thought Sam. It can't be true. The sheriff's really thinking about it.

'Well,' said the sheriff at last, 'I should send him back to jail, but I can't afford to lose a man to take him back. I suppose we could tie him up and take him with us.'

'He'd be a nuisance,' said the square man. 'Look, sheriff, I've known Abe Carter for a lotta years and they shot him for no good reason and now he's like to die of it. We'll get nothing out of this one and they'll only string him up after the trial.'

The circle of horsemen sat on their horses, leaning on their saddle horns. One or two had rolled cigarettes and were quietly smoking. None of them seemed concerned one way or the other. One of them even said it.

'Do one thing or the other,' he growled, 'and let's get moving. We're wasting daylight just talking here.'

One of the others had grabbed Straw's rein and was looking her over.

'Nice hoss this,' he said.

'Now if I were in this would I have a horse?' asked Sam, clutching now at anything that might be even a little bit in his favour.

'Yeah, tied to the back of the stage,' said the sheriff.

'Way I figure it,' said another man with a deputy's star on his tattered calfskin vest. 'He drove the stage here to dump it while the rest went on with the gold.'

'Yeah, that figures all right.'

Another man rode up. It seemed that the posse had been spread wide in its search for the stage. This man joined the group as yet another rider came along the track.

'Now listen,' said Sam, in despair. 'You got this all wrong from the beginning. Now ...'

Whatever he was going to say was never said. The latest arrival slid from his horse and pushed his way past the other horses to the front. He also wore a deputy's badge.

'Sam!' he called out as he walked forward. 'What are you doing here? You joined us?'

Sam's face lit up and he stood there with his mouth hanging open.

'You know him, Al?' asked the sheriff.

20

Al looked up at the sheriff in surprise.

'Yeah, I know him all right. Why—don't you? Met Sam in Narrow Bend coupla weeks ago. You remember, you sent me to collect that prisoner. Sam here was acting deputy and we had a good night in the saloon. He's a beer man. Whisky and him don't agree, I recall. He don't like it.'

Sam gulped and his first words had a hard time getting out.

'Al, am I glad to see you. I found this stage just standing here like nobody owned it and then these fellers turned up and they thought . . . Say, Al, am I glad to see that ugly dial of yours.'

Al grinned: 'Still the same old Sam.' He paused and then he went on more seriously, 'Maybe a good thing I did come along though. We're all taking it mighty bad about Abe Carter.'

'They were getting very serious about it,' said Sam, 'all these friends of yours. Anyway what is it all about?'

Al told him, with help now and then from one or two of the others; that the stage had been held up not far out of Wide Bend. The guard had been shot, the passengers herded out and the stage driven off.

'There was a big heavy chest of gold dust from Circle Mine,' went on Al. 'It couldn't be carried on horseback so we considered it pretty safe. It was only going to Bear Cross anyway.'

'Yeah, but they were cute,' said another man. 'Not only stole the chest, but took the stage to carry it in.'

'They must have had a waggon waiting not far from here, put the chest on it and away.'

'But away where?' said the sheriff. 'We got the pass covered, so they're this side of the mountain. They've got a hide-out somewhere, but where . . . still the longer we stand here the less chance we have of tracking 'em down.'

'Yeah, let's get on after 'em,' said the square man, Gordon. Sam couldn't help feeling that Gordon was feeling a bit disappointed about something now that Sam was in the clear.

'What about the stage?' asked Al.

'Yeah, we can't leave it here,' said the sheriff. 'But I can't spare a man to take it back. Only one thing to do.' He turned to Sam. 'I'm enlisting you as a deputy. Your job is to drive this stage to Bear Cross and hand it over to Ash Slade there. I'll see you later. Come on, boys.'

'But I can't drive this,' gasped Sam. 'I've never had anything to do with carts and coaches and such-like. I'm strictly a saddle-horse man. I'm not even trusted with a hay waggon.'

The sheriff wasn't listening to him.

'Ain't nothing to it, Sam,' said Al, grinning. 'All you do is get up on that box there, loose off the brake, shake the lines about, shout "HI, YI!" and off you go. Follow this bitty trail on out of these hills and you can't miss hitting the trail to Bear Cross. Nothing to it, Sam.'

The sheriff turned his head and looked sternly at Sam.

'I'm leaving the stage in your care. Get it to Bear Cross.'

With that he wheeled his horse and rode away.

Four

The posse followed and when the dust cleared Sam was alone again with the stage, six horses and Straw. Except for the still-falling dust he could easily have told himself that he had imagined it all, or it was just another dream brought on by last night's bad whisky.

He buckled on his belt and picked up his rifle. He found

22

that someone had tied Straw to the back of the stage. He went round and patted her.

'What are we gonna do now, Straw?'

But Straw did not care. She turned her head, snorted once and then stood waiting.

Yeah, what to do? Maybe the best thing would be to get on old Straw and ride like the wind away from it all. Just put as many miles as he could between himself and this stage-coach. And then again, if he ever did meet that sheriff again he didn't fancy facing up to him and trying to explain why he left the stage . . . well, he'd have a try.

He lengthened the rope to give Straw more room to move about and then went round to the front of the coach. He walked round the horses first. They were good horses in fine condition and there was an air of excitement about them as though they guessed that they would soon be on the trail again.

He climbed up on to the driver's seat and put his rifle in a sort of sling there that seemed to be made for it. Now there were only two things to worry about. Two things—the reins and the brakes.

He unfastened the thick leather reins and hauled back on them. To his surprise the two leaders began rearing. He eased off the brake and slacked off the reins. Nothing happened. He shook the reins and then remembered what Al had said.

'Hi, Yi,' he shouted.

The six horses set off at a fast trot, jerking the coach and throwing Sam against the back of the seat.

Too fast! He pulled on the reins and they slowed. There was nothing to it. Driving six horses was as easy as driving one.

After a few minutes of jogging along, Sam began to think that Al was right when he said it was no trouble. He looked back wondering how Straw was taking it. He was

23

pleased to see her trotting along with her head up, as happy as the six horses to be on the move again, but maybe not too happy about being tied.

The Fargo horses followed the narrow track without any help from Sam. He sat back and began to enjoy the trip. Driving was a good job after all. Maybe he should have tried it before. He'd heard it said that as drivers didn't usually carry guns, they rarely got shot by the road agents. He'd also heard that the pay was good.

Soon they came to the road that led through the pass. Sam saw this coming up and managed to turn the horses so that they were going down the road away from the mountain.

The coach rolled on making little noise apart from the clatter of the wheels and the clump of the horses' hooves. The sun was hot and Sam was feeling the loss of his Stetson.

It seemed to be no time at all before they joined the trail that led to Bear Cross. Everything was going fine, thought Sam. Maybe a bit too fine. He sat up straight in his seat and took a good look round. The horses seemed all right. What if Indians should show up. Perhaps he should get along a bit faster.

He shook the reins: 'Hi, yi.'

The horses lifted their heads higher and increased their pace to a fast trot. The coach rattled on. He looked back—Straw was keeping up well. No trouble there. This was great.

'Hi, yi. Hup. Hup.'

Suddenly, the horses were galloping. The trail flew under the hooves and Sam began to have doubts. What if a wheel hit a pot-hole or struck a rock in the road?

He pulled on the reins. Nothing happened! He pulled and pulled—still nothing. Then he guessed what had happened. The leaders had got the bits between their teeth, making the reins useless.

Faster and faster they went. The wheels whirled as the stage thundered on.

Straw! What about Straw? This speed couldn't be good for her, tied as she was. He lashed the reins on to the rail and looked back. Straw was galloping and keeping up well, but the rope bothered her and it showed.

Sam climbed on top of the rocking coach and inched his way along until he could look down at the rear of the coach. He took out his knife and put it between his teeth. Then he leaned over the back of the coach until he was half-hanging head-first over the back of the stage.

The trail flashed by below him at a rate that made him giddy. He grabbed the rope that held Straw and took his knife from between his teeth. He looked up. She was galloping hard. This was tricky—if she should stumble at this speed ... She was showing the whites of her eyes and there was foam around her mouth.

'Come on, Straw!' he yelled, for the second time that day. 'Up—come on ...'

He pulled firmly on the rope and she drew nearer. He did not want to cut the rope too near the coach and leave a long dangling length on Straw. A long piece of rope might get tangled in her legs.

'Come on, Straw, come on.'

Nearer and nearer she came until she was galloping with her nose almost within arm's length of the bouncing back of the coach.

That would do it! Sam slashed at the rope. The razor-sharp blade cut though it and Straw was free. She slowed and let the coach go on away from her.

The slashing of the rope almost made Sam lose his balance. He grabbed the coach side to steady himself. His knife slipped from his hand and fell into the whirling dust of the trail.

This has been a right day, thought Sam, as he scrambled back to the driver's seat. First his hat and now his knife.

The horses were galloping on not knowing or caring what was going on behind them. Sam looked back again. Straw had lost a lot of ground, but she was still coming steadily after the stage.

She had enough sense to stay some way back and to the side so that she kept clear of the stage's cloud of dust. She was all right. She'd follow all the way. Sam could now turn his mind to the stage and the horses he was *supposed* to be driving. He unfastened the reins and hauled back on them. He pulled with all his might. He braced his feet against the foot-board and pulled fit to crack his muscles.

Nothing! The horses went on as though nothing was happening. He gave up. The only thing he could do now was to hang on and wait for the horses to run themselves to a standstill.

The horses were enjoying their fast gallop. Sam looked up from them and saw that the township of Bear Cross was in sight. Not only was it in sight, but it was getting nearer at an alarming rate.

He tried once more. He pulled on the reins, but they could have been pretty ribbons for all the use they were. The horses seemed to be galloping faster than ever. At this speed, Sam and the two-ton coach would tear through Bear Cross and out at the other side like a little tornado.

He tried pulling on the brake, but that had no more effect than if he'd pressed his toe against the wheel. He looked over the side. If he jumped he'd probably break his neck or at least a leg or two.

For one mad moment he imagined himself jumping down on the horses' backs and working himself to the front along the backs of the galloping horses until he got to the leaders and then he could . . .

The first buildings of Bear Cross flashed past showing

only a glimpse of several startled faces. Then they were in the long main street. Buildings on both sides streaked by, chickens scattered, fluttering their wings and tossing away feathers as they fled. There were more people: men and women standing, watching, stopping what they were doing —the stage was here . . .

It seemed to Sam that everything in the town had stopped—except the stage. Then he saw a woman dash out to grab a child in the street. A man leapt out of the way of the great horses tearing towards him.

A quick glance showed a saloon and a big *Jail* sign. Still the horses galloped on. They hadn't yet crashed into anything and they hadn't run anybody down. Sam could only hold on and pull at the reins. At this speed they'd be through the town in the next minute. Sam could imagine himself a prisoner up on the swaying seat until the horses blew themselves out.

Then, without any warning, the horses slowed so quickly that Sam was almost pitched headlong on top of them. A moment later the coach had rolled to a quick stop. Sam grabbed thankfully at the brake handle and pulled it on.

He looked round. The horses had stopped the coach outside a long wooden shack with a notice at the front which read: *Wells, Fargo Office.*

Five

By this time people were running to the stage from all directions. Before the dust had time to settle, a small crowd had gathered round the coach with all their faces turned up to him. He climbed down amid a babble of voices and a hail of questions.

Most people wanted to know where the passengers were. Others asked why he had come in so fast. Then a short, heavy man wearing a deputy's badge bustled his way through the crowd.

'What's up? Never saw a stage come in so fast,' he said. 'Is it Indians? You being chased by Indians?'

'No, it's not Indians,' said Sam. 'Look, can I tell you all about it in a minute? I just want to get my horse.'

Sam pushed his way through the crowd away from the deputy who was then climbing on to the coach.

Straw! Had she got here? Was she still outside the town? Then he saw her. She was trotting down the street, not knowing where to go in all this crowd of people. One or two men on the board-walk were eyeing her, sizing her up—a good horse—straying ...

'Straw! Come on, old girl!'

At the sound of his voice she turned her head and trotted over to him. He untied the rope, checked his blanket-roll and found that she had not lost anything on the trail. He led her back to the coach and tied her to a nearby hitch-rail.

There was another man with the deputy. He was a tall, powerful-looking man with long straight fair hair and was about ten years older than Sam. He wore range clothes and a low-slung holster. He turned as Sam came back to the coach, then grinned and held out his hand.

'Hi, I'm the Fargo agent. Slade. Ash Slade.'

Sam shook the man's hand and looked him over. He liked what he saw.

'Sam Spencer. Glad to know you, Mr Slade.'

'Call me Ash. Maybe you'd like to come in the office, Sam and tell us all about it. This is Ed Watson.'

Sam shook hands with the deputy and they all went up the wooden steps and into the office. It was a business-like place with a shelf of files, a few bent-wood office chairs and

28

a swivel chair behind a black roll-top desk.

'Now what is it all about?' asked the deputy. 'We had it over the wire that the stage had been held up outside Narrow Bend and that it was missing. That was all we had and now you turn up with it.'

Having said his piece, the deputy was ready then to sit back and let Sam tell his story. Both men listened in silence until Sam got to the end of his tale.

'Seems you did well with the stage,' said the deputy. He turned to Ash Slade. 'Did you see him come in like a whirlwind, and then stop right outside the office.'

Ash Slade grinned at Sam.

'Yeah, I saw it all right.'

The deputy got to his feet and headed for the door.

'See you later. I'll take over the stage from you Sam, as the sheriff said—so your deputy duty finishes as of now.'

When they were alone, Sam got up and looked through the office window at the stage, where the horses were being led away.

'I got to go and see to my horse,' he said. Then he turned and grinned at Ash. 'There is one thing about the driving. I mean, I ain't as good as all that. When the horses stopped at the door . . .'

'It was because the leaders had the bits between their teeth. Yeah, I saw that, Sam. Don't let it bother you. You'd be surprised how many drivers leave it to their horses to stop at the right places. You had some good horses there. Anyway, it's not everybody who can manage a three-team hitch.'

'Yeah, well I'll be seeing you, Ash.'

Sam went to the door, and he had opened it when Ash said :

'Say, Sam, I guess the Company owes you something. You not only found the stage, but you brought it back as well. I can't give you cash, but maybe we could have a bite

29

to eat at the Company's expense—when you've fixed up about your horse.'

'Yeah, I'd like that,' said Sam.

It took Sam only a few minutes to get the ostler to take Straw into the stable for a rub-down and feed. He carried his roll back into the office. Ash was sitting at the desk. He got up when Sam came in.

'Leave your roll there, Sam, and let's go. We got a good eating-house here, but first I got another thing I'd like to do for the Company.'

'What's that?'

'I got to take you along and buy you a new hat. A man don't look right bare-headed round these parts.'

'That's a great idea. I don't feel rightly dressed without one. I guess some squaw is wearing mine right now.'

'We might even get as far as a knife as well, but before we go along to the store, what about a drink?'

'Sure thing, Ash, only find a place that sells beer as well as whisky.'

Later when Sam was sitting in the little eating-house with his new Stetson on the chair beside him and a knife on his belt, he began to feel that the day was ending a lot better than it began. He had got out of a tricky situation with the Indians and the stage-coach business hadn't ended too badly. What he needed now was money. When he'd paid for feed and care for Straw there wasn't going to be much left. He could either risk his last few dollars on gambling and hope for a run of luck, or he could try to make his money last out till he could find a job for a little while.

He decided on a job. He had been eating while he had been thinking about this and Ash, opposite him, was eating too. Ash smiled as though he read Sam's thoughts.

'Course, what you'll need now, Sam, is a job.'

'I was just thinking that myself. It's either that or cards.'

'Yeah, well what about taking a job with me?'

30

'You mean on the stage, for Wells Fargo?'

'Helping me to get this robbery business sorted out. Maybe even catch the stick-up artists.'

Sam gulped down a mouthful of hot food and wagged his fork in the air.

'No thanks, Ash. No more stage-coaches for me. I've had enough of stages to last me the rest of my days.'

'Oh, I thought you did well. I think you'd take to it very natural like.'

'I didn't think so at the time. No, it's not for me. I'd like to get me a job here in town, just enough to get a grub-stake together and then me and Straw'll be on our way. I don't mind spending my days in the saddle, but up on the top of that stage—never. Though I must admit that it cleared my head something wonderful!'

'Well, suit yourself, Sam, but I still think it would be just the job for you.'

They said no more about it and parted cheerfully. In order to save what little money he had left, Sam rolled himself in his blanket in the stable that night.

Around noon the following day, Sam again climbed the steps up to the Wells Fargo Office. Ash was standing inside by the open window.

'Hi, Sam, how are things going?'

Sam leaned against the wall outside the window, he pushed back his hat and looked down at the morning folk going about their business.

'You know something, Ash? Things ain't going too well and I need a grub-stake to get me to the next town.'

'I'll stake you,' said Ash. 'Just say the word and I'll be glad to grub-stake you out of my own pocket, if that's what you want.'

'Well, now, you see ... Maybe I'd better come in there. Easier to talk there.'

Sam turned and went into the office. Ash sat behind the desk while Sam sat astride a chair leaning his arms on the back.

'What's on your mind then, Sam?'

'I been thinking about that job you offered. Maybe there won't be much riding on a coach. Maybe I could help in other ways. Is the offer still open?'

'Well, now that you're interested, perhaps I'd better tell you a bit more about it. I'm here to try to stop these stage hold-ups and, as I said, I want somebody to help me on this job. You'd be a sort of Fargo detective or messenger. Then when I got this trouble sorted I'll be on my way too.'

'Where there's trouble, that's where you go?'

'Yeah, I've been lucky enough to get it sorted in a few places.'

'It wasn't luck the way I heard it,' said Sam. 'Everybody knows of Ash Slade. The way you handled the Cape gang in Yuma. I heard they used to rob the Deadwood to Denver stage nigh on every day, till you went there. They say ...'

Ash clapped him on the shoulder.

'Yeah, yeah, but don't forget your pinch of salt, Sam. These tales get better everytime they're told.'

'Maybe so, but even with a pinch of salt they're still great.'

'Well, what do you say about helping me out on this one?'

'Why me, Ash? You only got to go to the door and yell and there's a dozen young fellers, maybe good drivers, who'd give their left arms to work with Ash Slade.'

'Could be, Sam, but I asked you.'

'Count me in. I'll do anything you ask—even go on a stage.'

They shook hands on the deal.

'Right then, this is the problem as I see it. There's this Foley gang picking up a lot of gold in these hold-ups. As you know, they even went so far as to steal the coach to get the dust.'

'And they have a hide-out somewhere.'

'And it really is a hide-out. By the time the sheriff has got his posse moving, the gang have vanished. You've seen the foothills and the mountain? There are hundreds of canyons and hidden parks and valleys. Take six months to search the ones we can find, never mind the hidden ones.'

'What if the posse go along with the stage, or even trail it?'

'Then nothing happens. The gang's not fool enough to try a hold-up with the posse near. We can't always have the sheriff around. That's what I'm here to do, simply get this gang and make the line safe for normal traffic. First problem is to trail them to their mountain hide-out.'

'How we gonna do that? If we follow, they won't touch the stage. If we go on the stage they might hold it up, take it and leave us stranded.'

'Yeah, that's right, Sam, but what if we were already near the place where they hold up the stage? What if we got there the night before and hid out with the horses ready. They come, hold up the stage, take it away and we trail 'em right through the badlands.'

'Sounds too easy.'

'Simple plans often work best. Are you willing to try it out with me?'

'Sure thing.'

'We'll *make* 'em take the coach. The one we have is a good strong Concord so I'm gonna have the strong-box, with three stout locks on it, bolted to the roof. They'll never get it off in a short time on the trail. They'll have to drive it away. The fact is that I'm not sure they won't find it too hard to get off in their hide-out—less they got explosives there.'

'How do we know where to wait?'

'That's a bit of a guess. Now look on the map here.

33

There are two really good places for a hold-up—here and here. Now I favour this one, the nearest. That's the one we'll camp at tomorrow night, so let's keep our fingers crossed and hope I've picked the right one.'

Six

The next evening Sam and Ash rode out as twilight fell. Later as they followed the wide trail in the moonlight, they saw no-one and nothing that moved, except a few night creatures.

After a long steady ride they came to the spot which Ash had chosen as the first likely place for a hold-up. Rocks pushed their black fingers out of the sandy soil, rocks that gave plenty of cover. The high land on each side of the road meant there was no way for the stage to go, except between the rocks.

Ash said they would camp up on the high ground to the left of the road. They found a good-sized hollow that gave them a good view of the road and also cover for their horses. Sam had brought Straw while Ash had a pinto from the livery. They had also brought along a spare horse.

They left their mounts as far away to the rear of the hollow as they could. There was no question of them having a fire so they rolled themselves in their blankets to get as much sleep as they could.

'On jobs like this,' said Ash, 'you sleep when you can. There's no knowing when the next chance will come.'

Sam was wakened by Ash just before dawn. They ate a cold breakfast and then settled down behind the rocks to watch and wait.

The dawn glow in the east chased away the stars, as the black of the night fled leaving only the black of the rocks. Then the sun came over the edge of the world, lighting the long road that stretched away from the lonely clump of rocks across the wide plain.

They waited in a long silence. They lay behind the rocks while the sun climbed across the blue sky. The shade began to creep under the rocks until not much more than a lizard could have hidden in it.

Still nothing came, neither coach nor outlaws. Sam watched the narrow strip of road going east.

He gazed until his eyes began to make up little shapes that weren't there. He looked the other way. Nothing. He found it easy to think that they were the only two people left in an empty world.

Then it *was* there. The little tuft of dust that changed in a short time to six trotting horses, taking it easy as they always did on the road.

The coach came swinging along the road. The horses raised some dust, and more spurted off the wheels leaving a little cloud hanging behind them.

Then the horses were passing the first rocks. Soon they were between the rocks, twisting and slowing as the driver worked hard to keep the coach in the middle of the road.

Now was the time! Now was the moment for the hold-up men to leap forward. Now was the time for the warning shot. Now, *Now*!

Nothing happened. The coach went on between the rocks. The horses trotted out on the other side where the road opened out again.

Sam and Ash watched it rattle its way over the rocky, dusty road until—at walking pace—it vanished over a small rise.

Sam was about to get up, but Ash waved him down again.

'Better wait awhile,' he whispered. 'You never know what these fellers might be up to.'

They lay and waited and after only a few minutes it was as though the stage had never passed by. The road lay empty, the rocks shimmered in the hot air. A buzzard sailed in circles over the rocks.

'Come on, let's get our horses, Sam,' said Ash.

They rode slowly along the road with Sam leading the spare horse. Ash did not say much as they went along. They had to keep their eyes open for anything moving, a glint of sun, a cloud of dust or a puff of smoke.

The road wound its way round the base of the foothills, so they never got a long view of the road ahead.

Then the sound of one shot—faint with distance—cracked over the plain to them.

'Looks like we chose the wrong spot all right,' said Ash. 'Come on, Sam, no use hanging back any more.'

Ash led the way at an easy gallop, on the look-out all the time and ready for anything that might turn up along the way. But they met no-one.

Then they saw what they had been looking for—a small knot of people standing by the side of the road ahead. There was no sign of the coach. Minutes later, Ash and Sam pulled up their horses alongside the passengers and driver who stood silently waiting. A wounded man was lying on his side, holding his leg which had been roughly bandaged above the knee.

Ash dismounted and went to the driver.

'Is that his only hurt? Nothing more serious?'

'What happened, Charley?' asked Sam as he joined them.

Charley was a stocky man with a black beard and silver hair. He smoked a short clay pipe as black as his beard. It was soon clear that Charley was a man who took things calmly.

36

'They jumped us here,' he said, between puffs. 'I guess they reckoned Skinner was a little slow in throwing down his gun so they let him have one. Good thing it was a rifle and not a scatter-gun or they'd have got me as well. He ain't hurt over much though.'

Skinner, still holding his leg, looked up at Charley. He didn't say anything, but it was clear that he thought he certainly knew better than Charley on that matter.

'How many were there?' asked Ash.

'Six of 'em. All masked, but I reckon one of 'em was a Foley. Big feller, I seen him before. He didn't say a word, left all the talking to one of the others.'

'What then?'

'Weren't much to it after that. Skinner here fell off the coach when they shot him. Rest of us got down like a set of trained mice. Then one of 'em, a fat feller—only one without a rifle—he got up on the box and drove it off up the road. T'other fellers followed taking the spare hoss with 'em.'

Ash nodded.

'That's just as I expected it. The horses will follow behind the stage and cover any wheel tracks—least it'd make it harder to track 'em once they leave the road.'

Ash stopped and looked at the driver as though expecting him to say something else. Charley seemed to be enjoyhimself by just not saying it. He managed to puff his pipe and grin at the same time. Then he took out his pipe and spat, without looking, to his left. He paused and then said:

'I did as we said.'

'And they didn't see you?'

There were three more puffs.

'No, I turned to climb down, reached under the seat and pulled the string as you told me.'

Ash looked pleased about this, but Sam could not make head nor tail of what was going on. He was about to ask what all this was about when Ash said: 'Come on, Sam, Charley, let's get after them,' and went to mount his horse.

Seven

They turned their horses and went on up the road away from the grumblings of the stranded passengers. Sam felt sorry for them. After all they had thought this was a regular trip and now they had to wait for hours in the hot sun. And they would end up back in Bear Cross where they started. Still, there were other things to think about.

Sam rode up alongside Ash.

'What was all that about, with Charley here, I mean? Pulling the string or something. You two been up to some tricks?'

Ash laughed: 'Yeah, I guess it sounds like that, and I guess it's right too. I didn't say anything before 'cause I didn't know if Charley would be able to do it. We fixed it up last night, or I should say the night before last.'

'Work? What was there to work?'

They were riding along the road fairly slowly and they could see up to about a quarter of a mile ahead. Ash was keeping a good look-out all the time he talked. His eyes roamed the wild land around them.

'You see, Sam, the problem was that if they got the coach and took it off the road, maybe it would be impossible to track 'em over ...'

'Over the hard ground, like the sheriff said.'

'So, Charley and me fixed up a sort of track maker. Look down there.'

He stopped and pointed down at the road. Sam reined in Straw.

'Yeah, plenty of tracks, but ...'

'Look here, and there, and there,' said Charley, pointing his pipe.

Sam looked across at him: 'You mean the coupla black spots there?'

'And a few more further on.'

They rode on slowly and Sam could see black spots here and there along the road—spots that a rider would not notice unless he was looking for them.

'I get it,' said Sam. 'You've got something on—or maybe under—the coach, that gives out these black spots.'

'That's it,' said Charley. 'A can full of tar and oil mixed. I put a hole at one end, an air-hole at the top, and it lets out drops as it goes along.' He grinned: 'Maybe we can depend on that more than horse-droppings!'

'He fixed a plug in the hole . . .'

'And when the hold-up happened, you pulled on the string that pulled out the plug.'

'You got it, Sam. We coulda had it dripping all the way from Bear Cross, but we could only risk a little can and we didn't want it running dry.'

Sam grinned: he liked the idea. It gave a fairly easy trail to follow—you didn't need to be an Indian to follow this one—even though the drops were well spaced out.

There was really no hurry now. There was no need to go all out to keep the coach in sight, so that they could find out where it was being taken. Anyway, it would have got well ahead by this time.

Ash moved up ahead, but after only a couple of minutes he stopped and waited for them to catch up.

'Look at this,' he said. 'Starting to get more tracks here.'

They looked down at the road and, sure enough, the spots were getting more plentiful.

'Twice as many spots here,' went on Ash. 'Seems to start about here. Maybe the coach was going a bit faster and it shook it up a bit.'

Ash looked up the road and tried to think it through.

'No, it can't be that. The faster the coach goes, the farther apart the drops would be. Maybe they slowed here for some reason and that's why we're getting twice as many drops.'

'Wonder why they'd do that,' said Charley.

They went on, keeping a still more careful look-out. If the stage had slowed that much, it might even be stopped altogether. Maybe round the next bend, or the next, or the one after that. But there were no surprises round any of the bends.

Then, on a straight stretch, Ash reined in his horse and slid from his saddle. He walked a few steps along the road.

'Funny thing,' he said, 'no drops here.'

After a mile or so of a thicker trail of dots, suddenly there were none. Nothing! Just a little flurry of dots and then nothing.

Sam and Charley had ridden a little way ahead. They came back.

'Nothing at all up there,' said Sam. 'Not a single drop.'

Ash remounted and they rode on searching for the guiding spots. There was nothing. The trail had just ended.

'Maybe the oil ran out,' said Sam.

'That's not likely. I filled that can up.'

'Or the hole got blocked. That's more of a chance. Or they could have left the road. Could have struck ...'

'Not into that, Sam.'

Charley waved his pipe at the thick thorn and rough scrub that grew along the side of the road.

'Horses couldn't get through that.'

They rode on searching for the tiniest spot—nothing. There was no sign of fresh wheel tracks, there was just nothing.

'A coach can't just disappear into thin air, can it?' asked Sam. 'I still think the hole got blocked and the stage had gone on even though there aren't any tracks showing ...'

Sam stopped as Ash's big fist descended on his shoulder.

'We've been fools, Sam. Why didn't we see it? Now stop and think. Why did we get more of them drops down the road there?'

'Well, said Charley, 'the stage was going slower and so ...'

'No, another reason. Why should we get twice as many drops?'

'Because ... because,' then Sam grinned, 'because the stage went over the road twice.'

'That's right, it turned back. It doubled back on its tracks—just one of their little tricks in case we got a tracker after them.

Eight

They wheeled their horses and swung them into a gallop back to where the tracks ended. They got off their horses so that they could search the area better. Now that they had guessed what had happened, it was easy to find tiny signs that told them they were right. They could see now where the horses had gone off the road to turn, although the stage had stayed on the road during its turning.

'That fat feller can drive all right,' said Charley. 'He managed to turn them horses in a nice tight circle.'

'Come on,' said Ash.

They rode back further until they came to the place where the double trail of spots had begun. By this time many spots had been covered by the dust from the churning hooves.

'I think it was about here you got off your horse,' said Sam.

It seemed certain that the coach would head for the foot-hills.

'Here it is,' said Charley, pointing to two spots.

Once more upon the trail they went on slowly, not taking any chance of losing it again. Much of the way was hard flinty ground, and without the drops there would have been little hope of keeping track of the coach.

The trail led steadily towards the foothills. Soon it began to lead through a maze of gullies and canyons, and round fantastic rock formations. Sam began to feel hungry. Both he and Ash had eaten only a cold breakfast, but Charley had set off with a good hot meal inside him. Ash must have had the same thought for he stopped.

'We got plenty of time before sundown. Maybe we better stop and get a bite to eat,' he grinned. 'I can't see us being invited to supper when we catch up with 'em.'

They turned off into a narrow opening in the rocks which was almost like a roofless cave. Charley went in first and looked around.

'Seems all right,' he said. 'Just thought it might be a home for old Silvertips.'

'Don't say that,' said Ash. 'One thing we don't want now is to meet a grizzly who's suddenly got mad at being disturbed.'

Charley built a fire that burned brightly without smoking anything worth talking about.

'I can stop the smoke giving us away,' said Charley, around his pipe, 'but the smell from this bacon, not to mention the coffee, might travel for miles.'

They ate and then sat back feeling ready for anything. The horses trailed their reins and nibbled the short grass. There was no sound but the buzz of insects and the songs of the birds.

'I don't think this Wells Fargo business is at all bad if it's all like this,' said Sam.

'It ain't bad,' said Ash, 'but you can't count on this all the time. I guess we'd better get moving.'

Charley kicked dust over the fire and within two minutes they had cleared all traces of their visit. They went on following the trail of oil spots. Twice they lost the faint trail and had to spend time finding it again.

The sun was dropping down the western sky and the snow-capped peaks were throwing long shadows over the foothills and plains.

'We lose it once more and I guess it'll mean a night under the stars,' said Charley. 'We'll not likely find it again till morning.'

But they did not lose it again. The stage horses had gone slowly and the spots were fairly close together.

After a straight stretch that went across the side of the mountain, the spots turned up a long sandy slope studded with rocks. Ash stopped and drew back into the shelter of a rock. The others drew rein beside him.

'I have a feeling this is it,' he said. 'We'll leave our horses here and go a little way on foot. And we'll keep under cover as much as we can.'

They scrambled along between high rocks and sliding quietly over smaller ones until they came to a spot where they could stay hidden and yet see the whole of the slope. It was wide, and covered with small stones between the big rocks, like a ready-made road going up the mountain.

All was quiet and empty with only the sighing of a slight breeze.

'Gets narrower as it goes up,' said Sam, quietly.

Ash nodded and they all looked to the top of the slope which ended at the cliff-like wall of the mountain-side.

'Must be an opening up there if the coach went up,' said Sam. 'But there's not a sign of it from here. Looks a solid cliff.'

'Be a bit of a pull for them hosses,' said Charley.

'Our problem,' said Ash, 'is to get up there without being seen by anybody who's keeping a watch out.'

'Maybe after dark?'

'Maybe.'

They lay behind a rock and peeped over. It seemed certain that one man hidden in the cliff at the top of that slope could keep a whole posse at bay. There was no cover except for the widely-spread rocks, and the slope was too long for an open charge.

'There's nothing we can do in daylight,' said Ash. 'I guess it's as you said ...'

Charley, who had been gazing up at the cliff face, took out his pipe at this point and without taking his eyes from the cliff, he said:

'You know what I reckon this place could be?'

Sam and Ash looked at him in silence. They knew he didn't really want an answer. After another suck at his pipe, Charley went on:

'This could be the Nowhere Mines. They used to talk a lot about 'em when I was a youngster. I'll bet that's it— Nowhere Mines.'

Ash was interested.

'You think it could be, Charley? I know something about them, but I didn't know they could be here-abouts.'

'Why Nowhere? Sounds a queer name,' said Sam.

'Yeah, there were these silver mines, long time ago, kept pretty secret and not many folks knew where they were. Then the silver ran out and the canyon the mines were in sorta got lost for years—hard place to find, Nowhere Canyon.'

'Yeah, but why Nowhere?'

'Well, way I understand it,' said Ash, 'is that the canyon was right on the border. At that time they didn't know whether it was in Texas or New Mexico. Right on the border it was, so it was neither, it was nowhere. Ever since ...'

44

Sam gripped his arm.

'See that, Ash? Up on the cliff. There it is again.'

It was not much, just the glint of the sun shining on something in a dark crack in the cliff face.

'It *did* look like something,' said Sam.

'Sun shining on a gun? Could be, could very well be. Yes, I think this is it all right. Can you feel it in your bones, Charley? I'm pretty sure there's a guard up there. Let's get back to the horses, and keep your heads down.'

They crept back to where they had tied the horses.

'I'm sure this is it, Charley,' said Ash. 'Maybe this really is Nowhere Canyon. Do you think you could guide the posse back here?'

Charley took his pipe from his mouth and spat over a rock towards the valley below.

'With my eyes closed if you like,' he said. 'I won't say I could have found this hide-out in the first place, but now I've been here I can find my way back all right.'

'Reckon the best thing is you get the sheriff and all the posse he can muster and be back here, before dawn if possible, and then . . .'

Ash paused and Sam and Charley watched him in silence. This was Ash's show, he had to decide.

'Well,' went on Ash at last, 'there's no knowing how things will turn out. The biggest posse in Texas wouldn't get in there by charging up that slope, so me and Sam, we'll try to work something out. What we want to do is to get them to come out into the open, then once they're out a big posse should be able to deal with 'em.'

'How we gonna manage that, Ash?'

'I wish I knew, Sam, we'll just have to try to work something out as we go along. Best thing, Charley, is to tell the sheriff to set up an ambush round here and then wait for me or Sam to get a message to you.'

'Yeah, but what if . . .'

Ash waved his hand: 'What is they've got us prisoners,

45

or we're dead? Well, if nothing has happened an hour after you've got here, then the sheriff can do what he thinks best.'

Charley stuck his pipe firmly back into his mouth, mounted his horse, and rode off without another word.

Ash grinned as he watched him go.

'Old Charley ... they say he sleeps with that pipe between his teeth. Anyway, now we'd better ... Of course, I forgot something. Come on, Sam, we'd better stop Charley.'

Ash rode off after Charley with Sam following. Charley had not gone far and he turned when he heard them coming.

'I forgot,' said Ash, 'we're gonna hide our horses while we try to get in the canyon. You'd better come and see where we tie them up, then if things go wrong for us you can at least rescue them ...'

A little way back they were lucky enough to find a tiny park—a little patch of green grass nestling in the mountain rocks. It was well-screened, yet easily found again.

'We'll leave 'em here,' said Ash. 'You'll not forget them, Charley?'

'No,' said Charley and jogged off again down the mountain side.

Nine

They fed their horses with oats from their saddle-bags and then gave them water in the canvas nose-bag. After this they left them on long ropes tied to a stunted tree. Ash wound the rest of the rope round his waist.

'Might come in useful,' he said.

Then they each got out the worn leather jackets that Ash had said they would need if they had to stay out in the cold mountain night. Ash had got the jacket for Sam in place of the buckskin that Sam usually wore.

'That buckskin's fine,' Ash had said, 'but it sure do stretch if it gets wet.'

As they left, Sam looked back at the horses.

'They'll be all right,' said Ash. 'They can graze to their heart's content.'

The horses had been left saddled with the Winchesters in the saddle scabbards.

'We might want them in a big hurry and we can't carry rifles on this job.'

Sam began to wonder what this job was going to turn out to be. As they walked back the way they had come, he asked the question that had been bothering him ever since Charley had left.

'How do we get past this guard, Ash? That is if there *is* a guard there.'

Ash tried to look cheerful about it.

'If things go right for us, that shouldn't be too hard. After all, remember that people have got past army guards plenty times, and this lot will be nothing as good as the army.'

'You mean sneak in?'

'Yeah, sort of—we wait till it's dark.'

They crawled to the bottom of the slope and watched as the shadows grew longer and the night cold came creeping between the rocks. When the sun was gone and the stars came out, then the wind began to blow. They lay and shivered.

'I reckon we got an hour before the moon shows up,' said Ash. 'Maybe we'd better be starting out and getting as near as we can without being spotted.'

'How we gonna do that, Ash?'

'We do a crawl'n creep up the slope, making less noise than an Indian, till we get near enough to make a quick dash in when we get the chance. I reckon it'll be a box canyon with just that one way in.'

'What if we don't get a chance?'

'It's likely we will. Put yourself in their place, Sam. Maybe they do keep a guard all the time, but how often does anything happen out here? They get easy about things—bound to.'

'You mean fall asleep or something like that?'

'Maybe not as bad as that. I'm banking on using the change-over. Now it's ten to one that when this guard's time is up, he'll have to do one thing . . .

'Go and kick the next feller awake.'

'Right, and that's when we get in. It's only in the army you get the sergeant bringing round the next sentry. In out-fits like this more often than not the old sentry has to go out and hunt up the new one.'

'And that's when we sneak in?'

'That's it. Now we better take our boots off. Stuff 'em behind your gunbelt upside down. This is just till we get up there. Come, keep close, it's pretty black.'

Ash set off, bent double he glided from rock to rock. He was just a shadow in the dim star-light. Sam soon got the idea—fast and quiet between the rocks, then stock-still until the next sprint.

Soon they were halfway up the left side of the slope. Sam had found the going fairly easy, but the boots in his belt were digging into him when he crouched, and the rocky surface was hard on his feet.

Ash stopped and they crouched behind a rock and waited. There was no sign of anyone—no sign and no light.

Sam thought it could be that they were sneaking up a mountainside to a hole that was empty. They were creeping and dodging as though the whole Indian nation was up there, yet they had seen no-one and seen nothing except a sun-glint that *might* have been on a rifle.

He was about to say this, but Ash slipped on across an open space to the next rock. Sam followed, seeing Ash as just a shadow among other shadows.

On the second half of the slope Ash went slower. It needed only the clatter of a loose stone or the tap of a gun butt on a rock, and whoever was up there—if there was anybody up there—would know and be ready for them.

Then they were at the top—well to the left of where any gap in the rock face would be. Ash sank down behind a rock the size of a horse and Sam dropped beside him.

Ash put his lips to Sam's ear.

'Boots!' he whispered.

Thankfully, Sam tugged his boots on to cold feet. He felt so much better with them on.

They crawled nearer and then Sam put out a warning hand, but Ash had heard it too. It was a noise that told them they were right and that this was the outlaw's hide-out. Faintly, carried on the night wind, came the sound of voices—men's voices. It was like . . . then Sam realised just what it was like . . . it was like the noise that comes from inside a saloon. It was the noise you hear when you walk down a cowtown street on a Saturday night. It was the distant sound of a lot of men having a good time—men drinking and laughing and singing.

'With that noise in his ears a sentry is not likely to hear us,' whispered Ash, 'but it's better not to take any chances. Now what we do is wait. It's not likely anybody's gonna leave that party to stand guard until he's reminded about it.'

'So this feller will have to go and root somebody out.'

'Yeah, do you reckon we'll be able to see the entrance hole when the moon comes out?'

Sam could not guess and there was nothing they could do except wait, and hope that the moon would not be long. The air grew colder. They pulled their hats down, their jackets tighter, and sat patiently by the rock. They kept a look-out but they could see nothing except the shapes of big rocks. There was no shadow in all the darkness that looked anything like a man. Yet there must be a man—not far from them—an armed man who was ready to shoot at the least hint of an enemy coming at him out of the night.

Sam lost track of time and found his eye-lids dropping. In spite of the cold he dozed. Twice his head jolted forward and jerked him awake again. How much time had crawled by he could not guess. Then, at last, there was moonlight. It was not a full moon, but it was light. A silver light that chased away all but the blackest shadows. It was a light that should show them some of the secrets of the night.

Sam was now wide awake. What they had to try to see— what they *must* see—was the guard. Their eyes roamed the side of the mountain and then came back to the bottom again.

That was where the slope came up. There—that was where there should be a gap in the rocks. Then if the entrance was there, it stood to reason that the guard would not be far from it. Maybe somewhere round about . . . Sam saw him at the same time that he felt Ash's hand on his shoulder, telling him that Ash had spotted him too.

There was the faint shape of a man. Sam could just make out the sharp angles of elbow and knee and the straight line of the gun. It was the tiny shifting of position that had caught his eye. Moments later a couple of bits of soft slate rattled down.

The man was on a little rocky perch, a shelf of rock on the bare cliff side. He was still and silent again.

Ash and Sam waited in their shadow and stared across

50

the moonlit ground at the sentry sitting in his shadowed hole. They kept still, with only their eyes and hats showing above the rock.

They waited and the sentry sat like another rock on the mountain side. He sat so long unmoving that Sam began to think that perhaps the man was asleep. Maybe the sentry dozed on his rocky perch.

The cold lay over them. Twice Sam got the urge to cough. His throat tickled and he swallowed and swallowed, but it would not stop until he picked up a tiny stone and sucked it.

Then, at last, the man began to move. He got up, stretched himself like a cat after a sleep in the sun, and then slid down. As he hit the ground he cricked his ankle on a rock sticking up out of the sandy soil. He bent and held his leg for a moment and they could hear him cursing softly to himself before he went limping off into the darkness.

Ten

There was no need for Ash to whisper anything: Sam was only too ready to move off. They forced their cold cramped legs into silent action. They ran swiftly across the ground that lay between them and the cliff face.

The shadowed opening was there. Although it was wider than Sam had expected, it slanted into the mountain side in such a way that it hardly showed from a distance. Sam reckoned there was space enough for at least three riders to go down it side by side—or a coach driven carefully.

Ash got there with Sam close behind him. They stopped to look ahead through the gap. It was just a corridor of stone curving round to the right. The walls of the rocky corridor were smooth and high. Sam could see that once they went into the corridor, there was nowhere to hide if they met someone coming out.

Ash drew his gun and Sam did the same.

'Cover me!' said Ash.

He ran down until he got to the bend where he knelt on one knee and peered round the curving rock. He turned and waved Sam forward.

Sam ran to his side and they went on together. The corridor ended just round that bend and opened out to form a canyon. Sam had only a hurried impression of the wider, open space beyond the corridor before he found himself lying with Ash behind a rock.

They lay still, breathing hard and sizing up the hide-out. It was long enough for them not to be able to see the far end. Down the centre and to their right were several buildings. As far as Sam could see in the moonlight they were built of rock with shingled roofs.

'Looks like an old mining settlement.'

'I guess it's just as Charley said—these are the old Nowhere Mines. Must have got a lot of silver out of here in the old days.'

There were three shacks and a big barn standing a little way apart from the others. This building was open at one end and it was pretty clear that the outlaws' horses were stabled there.

'Probably built for mules way back,' whispered Ash, once more seeming to read Sam's thoughts.

The noise was coming from the centre shack. Lanterns shone through the uncovered windows, crossed blackly now and then as men moved in the shack. Sam looked up at the stars twinkling in the black sky that looked like a roof on the canyon. The moonlight lit up only the far end and here the shadows were deep.

Ash put a warning hand on Sam's shoulder. A man was coming along in the dark towards the entrance. This must be the new sentry.

Whether it was darkness or drink or both, the watchers did not know, but the sentry stumbled more than once as he went along the flat ground to the corridor. They waited until the man had gone past. They could not see him clearly, but Sam was sure that he was half-drunk as he lumbered along with his rifle at the trail.

Ash set off as soon as the man vanished down the corridor. Sam followed, watching where he was stepping and trusting to Ash to find the way.

They stopped at the first shack which was in darkness. Ash tried to see through the boarded window while Sam kept a wary eye out.

'Bunk-house,' whispered Ash. 'Bunks built right up to the roof—be packed like a chicken-house when it's full.'

The middle shack was the one that was lit-up and roaring, so they made a great circle round it to get to the far shack. This one, which was padlocked, they guessed to be the stores and cookhouse.

Next they crept towards the stables.

'Better watch it here,' whispered Ash, 'might be somebody sleeping on the job.'

When they got to the stables they went in slowly. The faint moonlight showed them that the outlaws had plenty of horses.

It was a long building containing three lines of stalls—one down each side and the other taking most of the centre space. Ash looked at some full sacks stacked at one side.

'Oats in most of these,' he whispered. 'Looks like Mexican beans in the others. They sure are well stocked.'

'Must be twenty–thirty horses in here,' said Sam.

'Yeah, and not bad ones from what I can see of 'em.'

Sam walked to the other side of the building where he

could see a big, bulky shape that was too big for a cart and yet somehow . . .

'Hey, Ash,' he whispered as loudly as he dared. 'Look here, I've found the stage.'

Ash came hurrying up to him. There it stood in the dirty stable, looking unreal in the faint moonlight. Sam thought how dead a stage looked without horses harnessed to it.

'Yeah, that's it all right, Sam. Pity we can't have a light. I'd like to have a look over her. Anyway first thing we got to do is give the whole canyon the once-over.'

They left the stables and crept back to the wall of the canyon. They were now some distance from the entrance. In the moonlight they could see beyond the shacks quite clearly.

'What's that?' asked Sam, pointing towards the back of the canyon.

There was a little outcropping of rock that partly hid the end of the canyon. Sam was pointing at a sort of reflection in the moonlight which made it look almost like . . .

'That's water, surely,' said Ash. 'That's the moon shining on water. Come on, let's have a look.'

They worked their way round away from the shacks, going carefully, hiding in every shadow, wary of every noise.

'This moonlight's getting nearly as bright as day down here,' said Sam.

Once round the outcropping they could see the closed end of the canyon.

'It's a box canyon all right,' said Ash. 'No way out there.'

'It sure is water right enough,' said Sam, for they could hear the water as well as see it. The moonlight shone on a pool of water as wide as a couple of cowtown streets.

'Pretty, ain't it?' said Ash.

The pool was fed from water that seeped from the canyon side. Instead of the expected hole and waterfall, there
54

was a long crack running the full width of the pool. Water ran from this crack in a thin trickle. The moon shone on the wide seepage making it like a sparkling curtain. Wild flowers grew round the edge of the pool.

'Like a silver river stood on end,' said Sam. He looked down into the pool. 'Wouldn't mind a swim in there. Be deep enough, I reckon.'

'Yeah, deep enough, but remember that's mountain water—you jump in there and it'd freeze your bones. Still, this is what makes this such a good hide-out—no problem about water. They got all they need here. There are not many spring-fed pools in these parts.'

'Not that they make much use of it for drinking, from what I can hear,' said Sam.

'That's so, if that was a pool of whisky, they'd all be swimming in it now.'

They skirted the pool and went to the other side of the canyon.

'Now what have we got, Ash? I guess these are the mines.'

They bent double, darted across the open moonlit space, and went to several black holes in the canyon sides. Slabs of rock and mounds of rubble were scattered around the holes.

'Yeah, they're the openings to the mines all right.'

Sam peered into one of the holes.

'All caved in, right up to the entrance. No chance of hiding in there. There's not enough room to swing a saloon door.'

They crept on to look at the other holes. There were five openings, all blocked solid with fallen roofs.

'Well, let's see what we've got now,' said Ash.

They had stopped behind a rock from which they could look out across the canyon.

'We got a box canyon,' said Sam. 'Only one way out.'

'And in.'

'And in, and that's guarded. Three shacks, a stable, plenty of water and a few blocked mine tunnels.'

'A dozen or more outlaws and their horses.'

'Yeah, and a coach with horses for it and who knows how much gold. You know, Ash, there must be quite a bit of gold in this canyon.'

'That's right, the last hold-up was nigh on forty thousand dollars and they had at least three smaller ones before that.'

They were near enough to the water to hear the endless trickle as it bubbled out of the mountain side. Above this sound came the drunken shouts borne on the cold night air. The stars, outshone by the moon, had paled to yellow sparks in a jet black sky. From far-off came the howl of a wolf.

Sam gave a sudden shiver and pulled his leather jacket tighter. Ash looked at him and grinned.

'Time for some action, Sam. Another coupla hours or so and the sheriff will be here. Let's get back to the stable. Maybe we can figure what to do there.'

They made their careful way back. It was warmer in the stable. The faint glow of moonlight shone on the backs of the sleepy horses. The building was full of small noises, from the rustling of straw to the chewing of oats. There was the smell of horses and leather mixed with the smell of lamp oil.

Ash stood and gazed at the black lump that was the coach.

'This is what it's all about,' he whispered, half to himself and half to Sam. 'The coach and the gold. Now if . . .'

He stopped and laid his hand on Sam's arm.

'Somebody coming!'

Eleven

Someone *was* coming. Someone was on his way from the middle shack to the stable. Then it became clear that there was more than one person. There were voices—two . . .?

Sam looked round, they had to get hidden, but where? For one wild moment he thought of getting in the coach.

'Up here . . .' whispered Ash.

He went into a stall, pushed his way past the champing horse and swung himself up behind the high manger.

The voices—and a swinging lantern—were almost at the doorway.

Sam pushed his way into the next stall and climbed up behind the wide manger. In a few seconds he had covered himself the best he could with the crackling straw. He moved one or two whisps which were intent on getting up his nose or into his ears.

He could still see about a third of the stable, including the part where the coach stood. A wooden partition stopped him from seeing into the next stall where Ash was crouched in the straw.

The lantern brought dancing shadows into the stable. The horses showed their interest by a general moving of hooves in the straw.

Sam tried to crouch even lower as three men entered the stable. One of them was a head taller than the other two. Sam guessed this to be one of the Foley brothers, who were the leaders of the outlaws. The other two men were carrying two boxes or chests between them. They had one box on top of the other and they held the handles of the bottom box. The boxes swayed as they carried them in and it was made clear, from the way they set them down and began rubbing their arms, that the boxes were heavy.

Foley hung the lantern on a nail.

As he turned, Sam got a full view of his face. There was a slit of a mouth beneath a hooked nose, and shaggy black hair hung below his hat.

'Right, let's get it loaded,' growled Foley.

The two men, blue-chinned and red-necked, looked surly and there was no doubt that they had not liked leaving the party to carry heavy chests about.

Foley opened the front boot. It had two doors that opened forwards. One of the chests was pushed in there and the door closed. The second chest was put in the boot at the back.

When this had been done the men stood there like sheep-dogs waiting for an order.

'All right, boys, you go on back,' came the Foley growl. 'I'll just check this out and then I'll join you.'

The two men swung round and were on their happy way back to the party within seconds. Foley did not watch them go: he was more interested in the gold. He opened the front boot again and looked at the chest for a long minute as though picturing its contents in his mind. He closed the doors and then climbed up to look on the roof. There was the big, iron-bound Wells Fargo chest still firmly bolted.

The forty thousand dollars, thought Sam. Foley was certainly very pleased with what he saw. He was like a miser counting his riches.

He climbed down and turned to lift the lantern from its nail. Then he changed his mind. He walked to the very stall where Sam was hiding. He patted the horse and pushed past it to check its feed. Sam held his breath. This must be Foley's horse.

By this time, Foley was not much more than an arms-length away from Sam. Surely he could not help seeing Sam crouched in the prickly straw.

Sam gritted his teeth as straw tickled his face, making him want to sneeze. His throat tickled, his toes felt cramped and his gun was digging into his side. He would have to move. He just could not stand it one moment longer.

But he did. He let out his breath slowly and kept as still as one of the trunk-like posts that held up the roof.

Then Foley happened to look past his horse's head, and he saw Sam. Even in the dim lantern light he saw Sam crouched there partly hidden by the straw. Instantly Foley's gun was in his hand.

'What the . . .' he began.

Sam rose on to his knees, pushed the straw aside and pretended to yawn.

'Hi, Foley,' he said, easily. 'How'r things at the party?'

'Who is that there?' asked Foley, peering up, his ready gun showing that he was not yet fooled by this act.

Sam rustled the straw, making a lot of noise.

'It's me—Ed. I just came for a sleep, just to get my head down for an hour.'

'Ed?' Foley paused, then went on in a more friendly fashion. 'Oh, Ed! Well, what's wrong with the bunk-house?'

Sam yawned again and stretched his arms upwards to show that he had no intention of putting his hand anywhere near his gun.

'Well you know how it is . . .' Sam suddenly remembered a name that went with one of the Foley brothers. 'Mart. It's quieter here and warmer. The horses warm thing up a bit. I'll just have another half hour. See you . . .'

Sam eased himself as though going to sleep again.

'Come out of that!' snapped Foley, his friendliness vanishing. 'Come on down here, I want to have a look at you.'

'Aw, Mart . . .' said Sam in a complaining manner. He really thought he was carrying off this acting pretty well.

Foley cocked his gun.

I guess that's as far as I go, thought Sam.

He climbed down clumsily, making all the noise he could. He pushed past the horse, following Foley who was walking backwards out of the stall. The tall outlaw was still carrying his gun so that it pointed in the general direction of Sam.

When Foley reached the end of the stall he stopped suddenly. He froze in his tracks like a jack-rabbit meeting a rattler.

The cold muzzle of a gun had come out of the dimness and had pressed itself into the soft muscles of his neck.

Sam heard Ash say:

'You don't want to die in a stable, do you Mart?'

Sam went forward and took the gun out of Foley's hand. He turned it and poked it into Foley's chest. He pushed on the gun, but Foley did not move. Ash removed his gun and Foley walked backwards to the open space in the middle of the stable.

'Now what is all this?' he growled. 'What's going on? This'd better be good or ...'

He then got a good look at Sam in the light of the lantern.

'Who're you? You're not ...'

He stopped as Ash, behind him, pulled his hands behind his back and began lashing them together with rope from a nearby saddle. Foley went into action.

'No you don't ...' he began to shout. 'Rab ...'

Sam hit him with the barrel of his gun. It was a short sharp blow just above the temple. The breath that Foley had just gathered for his shout, flew out of him like a big silent cough. He dropped limply to the ground.

Ash knelt, heaved him over and carried on tying his hands.

'Glad you were quick with it, Sam. Had to be done. They're not all so drunk they wouldn't have heard him shouting. That's it, now we'd better gag him.'

60

Ash tied the outlaw's greasy bandanna round the slack, open mouth and they looked down at him.

'Now what?' asked Sam.

Before Ash had time to reply, they were both shocked by a voice coming from the stable door.

'What are you doing out here all this time, Mart? They'll soon have drunk us dry back there if you hang about here any longer . . . say, what's that?'

Sam saw that a man had come into the circle of lamp-light. He was a short fat man with the beginnings of a bald head showing below his hat. He was not wearing a gun.

'You're just in time,' said Ash from behind Sam. 'There's been a little accident. Have a look at Mart here and see what you think.'

Both Sam and Ash had their backs to the lantern and their faces in shadow. Ash was looking towards the door, but no-one else appeared.

The fat man was looking down at Foley as he walked towards him. Then he saw the gag. He stopped and his hand went towards his mouth. Sam guessed they were not going to have much trouble with this feller. A fighter's hand goes down to his gun when he's startled, this man was no gun-fighter.

Sam held his gun in the light and pointed it at the fat man's belt buckle.

'Don't do anything you'll be sorry for. Shout . . . and you won't hear the echo.' Sam knew that he sounded like a fake saloon hard-case, but he guessed it was the sort of talk that would work on the fat man.

'Put your hands behind your back,' said Ash.

The fat man shot his hands back, his eyes fixed on Sam's gun. Ash tied his hands together with the rest of the rope. This one was certainly a weak sister. Already his fat cheeks shook as he gazed down at Foley.

'Is he dead?' he asked.

'Well . . .' began Sam.

'Yeah, he's dead all right,' broke in Ash, harshly. 'He wouldn't tell us what we wanted to know. A lot of good that's doing him now.'

Ash drew his knife and held it before the fat man's eyes.

'Now, quick, or you'll be like him.'

The man quivered, his eyes now fixed on the knife.

'What's happening?' asked Ash. 'Why has all the gold been put on the coach?'

The fat man's face was shiny with sweat in the cool air of the stable. He was ready to tell anything and everything.

'We're gonna take it out over the border. They fixed for Mexicans to break it open with nitro and hacksaws.'

'They'd never get it as far as the border. They'd be sure to run into somebody.'

A change came over the fat man's eyes. They grew bolder.

'I can take that coach and six over the border in two days. I know the roads, I been using 'em twenty years. That's why I'm here, that's my job. I might be useless as a gunny, but when it comes to driving a stage well . . .'

At that moment Foley began to moan and the fat man looked down at him and said no more. Foley wasn't dead! Then as Sam started loosening his bandanna, the fat man decided to become sly.

'Wait a minute, fellers, you want a share in the gold. I guess we could fix that. Come on up to the shack and meet the boys. We'll cut you in. Honest, you can trust me.'

Ash nodded to Sam who did his gagging act with the fat man's bandanna.

'Now what?' said Sam again, and they both looked towards the door. This time no-one came.

62

'I got the beginnings of an idea,' said Ash, 'but first we got to get these two out of the way.'

The fat man's eyes showed white above the bandanna when he heard this.

'Now where would you put 'em so they wouldn't be found in a quick search? Where wouldn't they think of looking first time round. I think I know.' Ash hauled Foley to his feet. 'You make that fat one walk, Sam.'

'Rope?'

'Yeah, we'll need some more rope. Bring that coil along. Sling it over Foley's neck and let him carry it.'

By the time they got to the stable door, Foley had recovered enough to be pushed along on wobbly legs.

Ten minutes later they had disposed of Foley and his fat driver and then they had a stroke of luck. It seemed as though things were going for them. Somebody up there was on their side.

They were creeping round the outside of the circle of light that came from the middle shack, when they heard someone coming down the rough narrow path that led from the entrance. They heard the man because he was singing softly to himself as he walked along carrying his rifle upside-down, holding the barrel and resting the stock on his shoulder. A happy man because his sentry duty was ended.

He went into the shack. Sam was for going on back to the stable, but Ash put out a hand.

'Wait . . . might be interesting.'

A couple of minutes later the door opened again and a voice said:

'The cold air'll sober him up—or freeze him to death.'

A man was half-helped, half-pushed out of the shack to stagger drunkenly along the path. He was carrying a rifle, but it could have been a broomstick for all he seemed to know about it.

Sam and Ash watched him reel away from the shack and out of the circle of light.

'Come on,' whispered Ash, 'he looks like easy meat.'

They crept after the sentry whose unsteady steps had taken him as far as the bunkhouse shack. Before Sam or Ash could get near to him, the man suddenly dropped his rifle and fell mumbling and moaning in the shadow of the shack. When they got to him the man was snuffling and snoring and giving in to drunken sleep.

'Like taking candy from a kid,' grinned Sam.

Within a couple of minutes they had the man tied and gagged.

'Right, let's put him with the others,' said Ash.

Ten minutes later, Sam tramped wearily back to the stables.

'Whew! I'm glad that's done. I collected a few fleas I think.'

'That ain't nothing to what we have to do yet,' grinned Ash. 'Wait till you hear the rest of my plan. And we've got to be quick about it, 'cause dawn ain't far off.'

'Yeah, that's true. Did you notice when we were coming back past the shack just now that things may be getting just a little quieter. Maybe some of them have drunk themselves senseless by now—like their latest sentry.'

'Maybe, but we can't depend on all of them being so obliging. I reckon they'll be up and roaring in an hour or so.'

They went over to a dark corner of the stable where they could still see both doors. They sat with their backs against the rough stone wall.

'Now,' whispered Ash, 'this is what we got to do next.'

Twelve

While Ash explained his plan to an amazed Sam, the moon still shone brightly over Nowhere Canyon. It shone on the shack where the lanterns still glowed. It shone on the mine entrances. It shone on the water and on the place where the sentry should have been keeping his lonely watch.

It also shone in at the open stable door as though reminding Sam and Ash that time was passing, and soon the sun would be rising for another hot day.

When Ash had finished talking they wasted no more of this precious time, but set to work on the second part of the plan. In little more than twenty minutes they returned sweating to the stable.

'I think I could just about sleep for a week after that,' whispered Sam, closing the door at the far end of the stable.

Ash went to the other door and took a look towards the middle shack.

'I'm surprised they haven't missed Foley by now and got a search going.'

'And the fat feller,' said Sam. 'Maybe the time has come for us to hide somewhere where we won't be seen. A search going on around here can make things a bit tricky for us. But we want to see if possible,' he grinned. 'I'd like to be able to see their faces.'

Ash considered and then looked up.

'The shingle roof's strong enough. They're not likely to see us up there if we keep in the shadow. They'll hardly be looking up there for Foley. Shouldn't be too hard to make a peep hole and see what's going on.'

'Yeah, that's it. So now all we got to do is move some of these horses and we can get up there.'

65

There were about twenty horses spread out in the thirty or so stalls. Sam and Ash began leading horses from the middle stalls and pushing them in others away from the centre. They filled the corner stalls, even managing to put two in some of them.

Sam stood in the middle and looked round at the empty stalls.

'That's good,' he said in a loud whisper. 'Don't seem half the horses here now. Looks like a few of 'em are missing.'

'Yeah, the empty ones show up more than the full ones. Well, that's it. Let's get climbing. We don't want to be caught with nowhere to go.'

They went out warily because they were then on the side of the stable nearest the shack. Sam climbed on to an old water butt and then to the roof. He leaned down to give Ash a hand up.

The wooden roof was one long slope and they crawled until they were about halfway up. As there were no holes in the roof, they had to do a bit of quiet chopping with their knives.

'Couldn't be better,' whispered Sam. 'We're over the right spot, so we might be able to hear what's going on as well as see it.'

They had left the lantern hanging on its nail which was low down on the pole and kept the light low. Through the holes came the warm smell of straw and horses.

There was nothing to see, so they lay and waited. They lay on their backs looking up at the velvet sky. The night wind whistled its soft way over the roof edges. Sam could just hear the faint, never-ending trickle of the water flowing into the big pool. An owl hooted and hooted, but got no reply.

Sam was thankful to be able to relax, even for a short spell. They had worked hard that night and it wasn't over yet. Would it all be worth it? Would it work. Would Ash's plan get the outlaws out of their hide-out?

He felt Ash's hand on his arm, and at the same time he heard the shack door crash closed. A man came shouting down the path. He reeled as he went along the little path that led to the stable.

'Mart, where are you?' he shouted, drunkenly. 'Where are ya? Come on, I've saved a bottle for you. Have you got Fatty with you? Have you got old Fatty?' He stopped and leaned against a post. 'Old Fatty!' He went on as though he was talking to the post. 'Old Fatty, he might be frightened of his own shadder, but he's the best driver in Texas.' He shouted, 'Fatty, you're the best driver . . .' His voice faded away to a mumble.

The man vanished into the stable, so Sam and Ash turned to their peep holes. They saw the man walk to the middle of the stable and stand there swaying and peering into the gloom beyond the lantern's circle of light.

'Mart, where are you? Where are you? Gone to sleep I reckon.'

He stood muttering to himself when there was still no answer to his shouting. Sam could look down on to the man's old stained hat, and he could just hear what the man was saying to himself.

'Maybe he's in the stage. Maybe he's . . . yes you're right, that's where he is, in the stage fast asleep. Fast asleep on all that gold. Don't trust nobody he don't. That Mart Foley, he just don't trust nobody, nobody at all.'

The man turned and walked a few steps towards the coach. Then he stopped and straightened up. Even from above, Sam could sense that the man had sobered. The happy drunken mood had suddenly vanished into the thick, lantern-lit air.

The man took two more quick steps forward and stopped, then he whirled round as though trying to catch someone standing right behind him. He stood half-crouching and looking all around the stable. With surprising peed he suddenly darted out of the far door, away from the shack.

The next moment he was back again in the stable, turning his head this way and that, as though he could not believe what he could not see.

At last he was convinced, and he ran through the doorway on the shack side, tugging his gun from his belt as he did so. When he was on the path, he raised his gun and fired two shots into the air.

Sam heard the quick restlessness that passed over the horses at the sound of the shots. For a few seconds this was all that happened, then the shack door burst open with a bang. Loud voices were raised as half-a-dozen or more men ran down to the man with the gun.

'Come on, come on,' shouted the man waiting for them at the stable door. 'The stage's gone!'

'What . . .'

'He's drunk!'

'And blind drunk at that!'

The men streamed to the stable and crowded in at the door.

'What's that matter with you, Jed?' shouted the first of them.

'I tell ya the coach ain't here. Go and look! It's gone—and the gold with it.'

The men pushed into the stable and then stopped and looked at the place where the coach had been. For long seconds they stood and looked, as though looking hard enough would bring it back.

Just below Sam was a figure that looked familiar. He had seen that fellow before, he was sure of it. Then he realised that it was the other Foley brother—Rab, that was his name—Rab Foley. He was much the same build as his brother, but younger and a bit wilder. Sam would

68

imagine the glaring eyes as he looked round the stable.

'If Mart's not about here,' Rab Foley was saying, 'then he must be outside seeing to the stage. He can't be far away.'

'I can't see anything out here, Rab,' said one of the men looking out of the other door.

'They can't be far,' Rab said again. 'There's Fatty with him. They've pushed the stage out to load it, that's what they've done. Go and look! Search the whole of the canyon. I'll get the rest of the boys.'

The men went out. Sam peeped over the edge of the roof and saw them spreading out to look in the different parts of the canyon.

'Hope they check that empty pole corral near the pool,' whispered Sam.

'I guess they'll surely do that.'

Once more Sam and Ash waited for something to happen. Rab and three more men came from the shack and walked into the stable.

'Looks like he's had to kick that lot awake,' Ash whispered, as the men shambled after Foley.

Hardly had they got into the stable before the others began returning from the search—all with reports of failure.

'We've been right to the end—nothing there.'

'Looked round the big rock, the pool and even the mines and . . .'

'You haven't looked everywhere,' shouted Rab Foley. 'You can't have. He *must* be there, the coach . . .'

'Honest, Rab, if you hid a deck o' cards out there we would have found it, wouldn't we boys? But that coach isn't there. No use getting frothy about it, it just ain't there.'

Foley kicked savagely at a piece of harness on the floor while the men stood and looked at him. Sam guessed that it was Mart who was the brains of this outfit. The men weren't used to looking to Rab for orders—and he wasn't used to making the decisions.

He aimed another kick at the harness.

'I need a drink.'

He grabbed the lantern and set off back to the shack, followed by the others—this being a decision that they all agreed with.

When all was quiet, Ash said:

'Come on, Sam, we'd better move them horses, just in case.'

They slid off the roof, landing in the soft, sandy soil. They led two horses each, to the pole corral near the pool. When they got back to the stable, Ash got two more.

'This way,' he had said, 'when they've had a think about it and they decide to do a count-up, they'll find the stage-horses gone.'

'And if they've checked the pole corral once they sure won't bother to do it again.'

While Ash was taking the last two horses down, Sam stayed in the shadow of the stable wall. As Foley had taken the lantern, the stable was dark, although much of the outside was still lit by moonlight. Sam leaned against the corner of the stable where he could keep an eye on the shack. Things were going fine. Everything was going according to plan. He was getting used to being in the middle of the outlaw gang in Nowhere. They'd got three of them already—get a few more and they wouldn't need the sheriff.

He went to the other corner of the stable where he could look out for Ash coming back up the track. He was beginning to feel hungry. Had they any food left in their saddle bags? He couldn't remember . . .

A gun was jabbed painfully into his back and a voice said quietly:

'Put your hands up, mister, then keep mighty still, or . . .'

Thirteen

The gun jabbed harder. Sam put up his hands, the sudden shock of it had set his heart beating wildly. Yet his first thought was for Ash. He would be coming back up the track any second now . . .

He felt his gun being taken from his holster. What could he do—jab his elbow back at the fellow's head—kick back at his shins—maybe . . .

But he knew that you can't get away with that sort of thing when a loaded and cocked gun is pressed tightly against your spine—and a stranger's finger on the trigger.

'All right, move!' the voice said, and the muzzle insisted.

Sam walked forward into the moonlight with his hands still raised. As he got near the stable door he saw Ash coming up the track towards them.

Ash was coming warily and he saw Sam and his captor at exactly the same second that they saw him. Sam felt the muzzle of his own cold gun pushed against his cheek. The man was holding Sam's gun in his left hand—plain for Ash to see. Ash stopped and then stepped quickly sideways into the cover of rock-shadow.

'Hold it!' the man said, loudly. 'You behind there, come out with your hands up or he's dead.'

The man jerked Sam round so that Ash could not fail to see the gun pressed against Sam's head. Sam knew there was nothing that Ash could do—not one thing.

A moment later, Ash came out into the moonlight with his hands raised. As he walked towards them, Sam noticed that Ash was not wearing gun or belt.

The man stepped away from Sam. He had a gun in each hand and he stood where he could easily see both of them. He was a short, squat man with a square beard that glowed a foxy red in the moonlight.

'All right,' said the man. 'Round the side here and take it easy to the shack. Don't do anything to make me nervous.'

Sam had hoped that they would go through the stable, but on this side of the stable was bright moonlight. Ash led the way, Sam was a little to one side and the man followed warily behind. Sam glanced at the man out of the corner of his eye and thought less and less of their chances of escaping from him. His face was set and the guns were rock-still in his hands. This was a lot different from dealing with an easy Fatty.

It took them only a couple of minutes to get to the shack door. Noisy, rough men's voices, came through the rough stone wall.

'Open it up!' ordered the man.

Ash lifted the latch and swung open the door. He paused, but there was nothing else for it, they had to go in. He stepped into the lantern-lit shack and Sam followed.

Their appearance stopped the talk dead for a couple of seconds. Then noises of surprise rose as the red-bearded man followed them in, his two guns still ready in case there was a break for freedom by his two prisoners.

'What you got here, Griff?' asked Rab Foley. He came forward from the end of the shack with a whisky bottle in his fist. 'Where'd you get these?'

Sam looked round at the bearded faces of the men and could not help a little shiver going through him. Things had suddenly all gone wrong. He had a picture in his mind of Straw tied to the stunted tree.

Ash had put down his hands, so Sam did the same.

'Caught 'em sneaking round the stable,' said Griff. 'Leastways, this one was round the back and t'other coming up from the pool.'

'All right, who are you and what are you doing here?'

snapped Foley. He raised his fist as though to hit Ash. 'Spill it!'

Ash took a step backwards, his forearm raised in front of him.

'We ain't done nothing, mister,' he said, in a meek and frightened voice. 'We're just a couple of cowpokes riding the grub-line. Ain't intending any harm and sure ain't done none as far as I can see.'

Griff had closed the door, holstered his own gun, and now he threw Sam's gun on to the table. Sam looked at the gun, but knew there was no chance of getting it. They would have to try to bluff their way out of this one.

Foley poked his head forward: 'What'ya doing here in Nowhere?'

'I told you,' said Ash, talking fast—as a frightened man would. 'We're looking for work—just drifting—then some Indians spooked our horses coupla nights since and got away with 'em. And we been walking. We rested in daylight and walked at night. Too hot . . .'

'Yeah, really was hot!' put in Sam.

Foley turned to Sam.

'How'd you get in?' he demanded. 'Nobody gets in here without our say-so. How'd ya get past our guard?'

There was a short silence. Everybody looked at Sam.

'Guard?' he said. 'There was no guard. We just walked in.'

Rab Foley looked across at Griff.

'Was the guard checked when we looked around? Who was it?'

'Pete, I think. I'll go look.'

Foley stared at Sam again as his slow brain tried to reason all this out.

'But what gets me,' said one of the other men, a long, lanky fellow lounging with feet sprawled. 'What gets me is how they knew to come in here in the first place. How'd they know it was here? There's no way of telling from the outside. That's why Nowhere gets lost every so often. That's what I want to know. How'd they know it was here?'

The long, lanky man stuck an unlighted cigar back into his mouth and showed his teeth round it as though to say—that's done for 'em.

Sam thought quickly: his brain raced round and round looking for an answer. Maybe they'd been told by an old friend . . . maybe they'd lived here once . . . maybe when he was a boy . . . maybe it was just an accident . . . maybe . . .

But Ash was looking across at the lanky man with eyes that were wide and innocent.

'Nor would we have known,' he said, 'if we hadn't seen the stage come out. There was us tramping past when this stage with a three-team hitch comes tearing out of the cliff. Put the wind up us for a minute. Wouldn't have minded a ride on it, but it went on like the wind. We thought it funny, so we come on up and found the opening and . . .'

He trailed off his words as everybody looked at him in shocked silence.

'You *saw* the stage leave?' hissed Foley in disbelief.

'Yeah, I just said . . .'

'When . . . when was this?'

Ash screwed up his eyes as he considered, making Foley fume at his slowness.

'Not more'n twenty minute since, I guess,' said Ash, at last. 'Maybe a bit less . . .'

Sam made a quick reckoning. It was nicely put. That would make the leaving of the stage as not long before it was first missed.

Foley was still thinking about this when the thin, lanky man took out his cigar again.

'That means they can't have got far. We could catch 'em

if we got a move on and if,' he looked round at all the others, 'if we all want to catch 'em.'

Foley's eyes narrowed. This was something he *could* understand.

'You mean I'm in with all this making off with the gold. You suggesting that, Jack, then get up and say so.'

'I'm not saying that, Rab,' said Jack, staying exactly where he was, 'but if we did go after 'em in a bit of a hurry, it would prove something now, don't you think?'

Foley looked round at them all.

'Right, then let's go. Come on, get the horses out. I'll show you whether I'm with 'em or not.'

'What about these two? What'll we do with 'em. Maybe we'd better blow out their brains and have done with it.'

Foley paused to look again at the prisoners. Sam knew that their lives rested on Foley's decision.

Fourteen

Three things got together to save them. One was that Rab Foley took such a time to make up his mind about anything. Another was that the thin, lanky man said to Ash:

'Ain't I seen you some place before? I think you should find out about this feller, Rab. Seems to me he ain't all he's set up to be.'

Rab Foley stared at him, his mind now turned to this new subject.

'Yeah?'

The third thing was Griff coming back with a rush into the shack.

'It was Pete supposed to be up there. You recall he went out pretty drunk. Well, he ain't there now. Nobody on guard there at all, so he's either sleeping it off behind a rock somewhere or he's gone on the stage. I just checked the stable now and all the stage horses have gone. It's nigh on dawn, but too dark to pick up any tracks yet. We gotta get moving, if we've to have any chance of catching 'em.'

'Right,' said Foley, now all in a rush to get on the trail. 'Take these two into the stable and tie 'em up, but good. We need a coupla men to stop behind, stop anybody else wandering in. Maybe Jack was right and there is something fishy about this feller. We'll have it out with 'em good and proper when we get back.'

'Right, come on!'

Sam and Ash were hustled and pushed and jostled back along the path to the stable. There Griff searched them while the lanky man held a gun on them, and the rest of the men were in the hurry and bustle of saddling their horses.

Griff took everything from them. Their pockets were emptied and Sam's gunbelt was stripped off him.

'Make sure there's no chance of 'em getting free,' shouted Foley from the other side of the stable.

'Don't worry, Rab,' called back Griff. 'I tie 'em quick, and when I've tied 'em they stay tied.'

Sam and Ash were pushed down on the ground with their backs against the trimmed trunks which were two of the main supports of the roof. These posts were about three feet apart.

In double-quick time Griff tied Sam's hands behind the post and then wound a rope several times round his chest. Then, cutting off more pieces of rope, he treated Ash in exactly the same way. When he had done this he was breathing heavily, but clearly very proud of his work. He cut the knots close, threw down the bits of rope, stood back to look at his prisoners, and grinned across at Jack who had watched it all.

76

'When I tie 'em, they stay tied.'

'You sure do a pretty job,' said Jack. 'It's a pleasure just to watch you. And there's no mistaking they'll stay tied all right.'

Sam was inclined to agree with him. The ropes were tight; the close-cut knots would never slip. He sat with back against the rough trunk and already he could feel his fingers swelling. The rope was tight around his chest. He felt like a blanket roll tied to a saddle.

'Come on, come on,' shouted Foley. 'Every minute counts. They're putting ground between us all the time.'

Sam could see through the open door that the sky was lighter in the east. The shadows were getting thinner by the minute and the pre-dawn light was over all the canyon. Maybe it was because of the fast-coming dawn that Griff did not notice the pale light of a lantern hanging on a post near Ash. If Griff had put out the light he would have left them in the semi-darkness of the stable.

There was a great clatter of hooves as the gang left, and Sam and Ash were alone with a few restless horses.

Sam stretched out his legs, bent them, and then stretched them again. This was the only movement he could make, apart from turning his head from side to side. The coils of rope were tight round his chest, his wrists were tightly bound together, and his hands were hot and swollen.

He looked across at Ash who was quietly testing his ropes. It was clear that they were just as tight as Sam's.

'How we gonna get out of this, Ash?' Even as he said it, Sam thought what a stupid question it was. Here they were sitting on the ground with their backs against strong posts, their hands were tied behind the posts and the rope was wound tightly round their chests—and also tied behind the posts.

How *could* they get out of it?

The tops of the posts held up the roof and the bottoms

were firmly fixed in holes in the ground. The ropes, though not new, were strong enough to hold the strongest man without breaking. Their legs were not tied together, but the ropes around their chests were too tight to allow them to stand.

Sam flexed his muscles and tried to move, but even the slightest wriggle under the rope seemed impossible. He looked across at Ash who was watching him closely.

'Well, any ideas, Sam?'

Sam looked round for something that might help. The dawning light shone faintly through the open door. It was not enough to see anything plainly by, but the faint, flickering lantern helped. Maybe the lantern light would shine on something . . .

There wasn't anything that could be of the slightest use to them—no sharp pieces of metal, no broken glass or sharp pieces of flint, not even on old nail sticking out of a piece of board. There was nothing but trodden ground, whisps of straw from the stalls, some bits of rope and a few splintered pieces of rotting wood.

That was all he could see. If there was anything else it was too far away to reach anyway. The thin, lanky man, Jack, had grabbed Sam's new knife, while Griff had taken Ash's. Their pockets were empty.

Sam could think of nothing else. There was no way to get free. The whole thing was impossible.

He could hear horses moving in their stalls at the back of the stable. He could hear them champing—they had sharp teeth—they could soon chew through a rope. Now *if* Straw were here, and *if* he had trained her to bite rope then . . . Maybe if they wore sharp spurs—but they didn't.

Ash was slowly trying to move. He was trying to squirm himself downwards. Sam noticed that Ash had fastened up his old leather jacket before he had been tied. Sam had left his open. Not that . . . but then Sam saw that it *did* make a difference.

78

Ash was trying to move his body down inside his jacket. The ropes were tight around him, but they bore hard on the jacket and he was able to move just a little inside it. The jacket ruffled itself further and further up his chest.

Of course, that was it, thought Sam. Ash will wriggle down until the ropes are just a little bit loose and then . . .

But Ash had got as far as he was likely to get inside the ropes. His great effort, which had brought sweat standing out on his forehead in the cold morning light, had helped him to wriggle down maybe two or three inches, but that was all.

Ash lay slumped against the post, still firmly tied and with his long legs stretched out before him. It must have been a huge effort to get even that far.

Sam's heart sank. If Ash couldn't make it, there was no hope. He strained against the ropes again. If only he had something . . . anything would do. But Ash had not given up. He was moving his legs around on the floor as though gathering something up. What was the idea now?

Then Ash stretched out as far as the ropes would allow and raised one leg slowly. He lifted it with his foot pointed, straining until it reached the short post nearby, on which the lantern hung. The toe of his boot just touched the bottom of the lantern.

In the brightening dawn light, Sam could see the strain on Ash's face, the sweat running down his cheeks. Then Ash tipped his foot up just a quick final couple of inches. The lantern bobbed off its nail and tumbled down to the hard floor below.

As it toppled, some of the remaining oil spilled out, catching alight as it did so. Some of the oil splashed on Ash's levis, lighting them with a low spreading, yellow flame.

Ash rubbed one leg over the other to put out the burning spots of oil. The rest of the oil that had reached the ground, spread and began to soak into the dust. Some of it

79

caught alight, making a little sea covered with tiny dancing flames.

Ash pushed hard again with his feet and then Sam could see what he had been scraping together before he had knocked down the lantern. He had been gathering together some of the short bits of rope that had been cut off by Griff. Now he pushed the rope into the flames.

The oil had almost burned away and the flames flickered weakly, but the rope caught alight. Tiny spouts of flame shot out as the whiskery threads sticking out of the rope burned away.

Then, in less than a couple of minutes from the fall of the lantern, it was all over. There was only the cold dawn light left when all the flames had vanished. Sam now could see what all this had been about.

One of the pieces of rope still glowed red at one end. It lay on the floor burning like a long, fat cigar.

This was what Ash wanted. He moved the rope with his boots until it was firmly caught between them. Then he carefully lifted it up.

The rope, glowing at one end, rose into the air between Ash's dusty boots. Slowly, Ash twisted his body so that his feet swung towards Sam, the rope gripped between the sides of his boots.

He'll never do it, thought Sam. No matter how strong he is, he surely can't twist round far enough.

Then it fell! The rope slipped from his boots and dropped, scattering little sparks on the ground. Perhaps the glowing end had dropped off—it would be impossible to light the rope from it again.

Ash began pushing the rope back into the position where he could try it again—the end still glowed. Sam held his breath when once more the rope hung with a little black whisp of smoke coming from it.

Nearer and nearer it came until the glowing end was
80

pushing gently against the rope around Sam's chest. Ash's boots were digging painfully into Sam's side, but it was working—the rope still smouldered.

Sam could see that Ash had to be gentle in his movements. If he pushed too hard, the glow would be gone. He held it steadily, though sweat ran down his face with the effort. Then smoke from the *two* glowing ropes rose in little spirals, making tears stream from Sam's eyes. He strained forward as much as the ropes would allow.

'Not yet, Sam,' gasped Ash. 'Hold it a minute.'

Bits of glowing rope dropped off. Sam had to close his eyes and leave it all to Ash. Soon, above the harsh smell of burning rope came the smell of scorched leather.

Ash dropped the rope from his boots. He no longer needed it for the rope round Sam's chest was glowing brightly. Sam put his head down and blew on the smouldering rope. At the same time he strained his chest against it. He heaved and heaved—and then it broke. The rope parted, scattering sparks that died blackly as they reached the ground.

Although he had rid himself of the rope around his chest, Sam's hands were still tied behind the post. Not free, but halfway there.

'That's great, Ash. Better take a breather before we have a go at the other rope.'

But Ash had no time for resting. He pushed a piece of burning rope with his feet until it was near Sam's post. Sam found that he was able to squirm round on the floor, working his way round the post until his hands were near the piece of burning rope.

Ash had the difficult job of pressing the glowing end to the rope around Sam's wrists. Several times Sam winced as the burning rope touched his hands.

Sam pulled again and again, and then his arms jerked and he was free. He rose to his feet and began stamping

81

out the glowing bits of rope. He grinned across at Ash as he rubbed his wrists and flapped his hands to get the blood moving again.

'When I tie 'em, they stay tied,' he said.

Fifteen

It wasn't long before Ash was rid of his ropes and dancing around to get his blood circulating. Ash had run out of the stable door to the rock where he had stopped when Sam had been caught. He returned to the stable buckling on his gunbelt.

'I guessed it,' said Sam.

Ash grinned. 'When I saw that feller had the drop on us, I dropped my gun at that rock. Lucky he didn't spot it.'

'Quick thinking.'

'Now, I think the first thing we've got to do is get Fatty. We have a little job for him to do. And bring some rope, some of that hung up there.'

Five minutes later they were pushing Fatty up the path that led to the entrance. Ash jabbed his gun into Fatty's back.

'Listen, Fatty,' he said, in a voice rougher than Foley's, 'it's gonna be a nice sunset tonight. Now if you want to see it, you do exactly what I say. You got it?'

Fatty set his cheeks shaking round his gag as he nodded. Ash untied the bandanna.

'I want you to say just what I tell you. Get it? You might not like it. You might think it's not a nice thing to do, but if you don't . . .'

He jabbed the gun into Fatty's back.

'If you don't, then something not nice is going to happen to you. All right?'

'Yeah, all right, all right, anything you say, but don't keep jabbing that thing in my back, it might go off. Anyway it hurts.'

Ash winked at Sam from behind Fatty's back.

They went on quietly until they were at the entrance, below the place where the guards would be posted.

'Now, Fatty,' whispered Ash, 'I want you to shout to whoever is up there and get them to come down here. We'll be behind this rock and if you make one little move, one little mistake, somebody will have a very big hole to dig. Get it?'

Fatty shook his cheeks again. The sweat of his fear ran down his face. Ash and Sam ducked down behind a nearby rock. Fatty stood doing nothing.

'Go on,' said Ash, in a loud whisper. 'Shout!'

Fatty looked wildly round, but there was no escape.

'Hey, up there,' he called, 'who's—who's up there?'

They waited, but nothing happened.

'Louder!' whispered Ash.

Fatty cleared his throat and gulped a breath.

'Hey, up there. Who's there? It's me—Fatty.'

A minute passed, and then there was the sound of boot on rock. Sam saw the shine of a rifle barrel up among the rocks. Another minute passed. Fatty was breathing heavily as though he had been running.

'Who's that?' came a voice from above.

'It's Fatty.'

There was another pause, and then some whispering.

'Fatty?'

'Yeah, come on down. Mart wants to see you.'

'Yeah, but . . .'

'Come on.'

'Tell them you've got the gold,' whispered Ash.

'Come on, we got the gold here. We need your help with it.'

It was the use of Foley's name that decided the men above. They came scrambling down the rocks to Fatty, who stood there with his big round face turned up to them.

Sam guessed that the two men were more than likely bored just looking out on an empty landscape, and wondering if maybe they were missing all the fun. Now it seemed that something interesting had turned up on their doorstep.

They jumped from rock to rock, keeping their balance with their right hand, and carrying their rifles in their left. They arrived almost together at the bottom rock to jump down the last few feet. They landed not far in front of Fatty who still stood without moving.

'What's all this about then, Fatty?' asked one. 'We thought . . .'

'All right, stay just where you are. Don't move!' snapped Ash, as he stood up from behind the rock pointing his gun. 'Put your hands up!'

The two men, completely surprised, slowly raised their hands. One of them, with tangled beard and ragged hat, looked across at Fatty and spat on the ground.

'You yack!' was all he said.

Sam stepped out quietly from behind them and took the rifles out of their hands. These he threw on the ground and then snatched their pistols out of their holsters. Both had Colts with worn wooden grips.

'All right, now over here.'

Ash waved the three men over to a flat space amid the rocks. There, while Sam held a gun on them, Ash quickly tied all three, wrists and ankles.

'We'll leave 'em here for the time being,' said Ash. 'No need to gag 'em, they can make all the noise they like now.

We got to get up there in case the rest come back pretty quick. There's no knowing how long they'll be, but I'd guess it'll be soon.'

They took the two Winchesters and the six-guns and climbed to the top of the look-out rocks. There was a magnificent view of the wild landscape stretching out to the hazy horizon. Cacti grew among the stubby rocks. Here and there, scrub oak trees were changing colour, bringing touches of red to the yellow land.

The low sun made shadows as black as the rocks, and the rugged country lay under the wakening day as empty as it was before men came to it. Birds had wakened and flew from rock to rock, testing the morning and singing its praises.

Sam and Ash settled on the rocks as comfortably as they could, ready for whatever might happen. Sam lay with his Winchester lying near and his six-gun in his holster. The spare six-gun lay next to the rifle.

'The only thing is,' said Ash, who was sitting with his back against a rock, 'we ain't got any spare rounds for the rifles. Seems like they weren't expecting a lot of trouble. What you got in yours, Sam?'

'I got a full magazine. Fifteen shots.'

'And I got sixteen. I guess this feller believed in his Winchester being a 'sixteen-shooter' like the old Henry. He's got one up in the chamber as well.'

'So we got none to waste.'

Silence hung over the mountain, and after a while when the sun was higher and brighter and hotter, Sam thought of the cold mountain water dribbling into the pool. His lips got drier every second. He was about to suggest that he should go down and bring up some water, when Ash grabbed his rifle and lay down on the rocky ledge.

'There's something!' he said.

Faint in the air came the crackle of far-off shooting.

There was a short flurry of shots, then a few spaced out, ending with single reports—a crack-crack every few seconds.

'Sounds as though they've found something else instead of a stage-coach,' said Ash.

'That's the sheriff and his posse?'

'Yeah, and I guess it'll be a big posse this time. He should have rounded up everybody from Wide Bend, Narrow Bend and Bear Cross—everybody who can shoot that is. Should make at least forty riders and they'll take some stopping once they get on the tail of this gang. I'll bet that Foley and his crew are pushing their horses now to get back here.'

'So when they get here . . . ?'

'When they get here, Sam, we stop 'em from getting back into the canyon. Once inside they can hold out against a dozen posses.'

'We just hold 'em off.'

'As we ain't got much in the way of ammunition for the Winchesters, we can't have a long shooting match with them. I'm hoping we won't need to. The sheriff will be close. All we got to do is stop 'em. They'll be running hard and it won't be easy. Maybe we could do it by giving 'em a shock.'

'It's gonna be that all right.'

'Yeah, they'll be thinking they've made it and they're just about on their home ground, and it's at that point we give it to 'em.'

By this time the firing was less, but louder.

'Sounding more like a running fight now,' said Ash. 'Now when they get here, if we both fire together at the right time, they'll get down under cover. We want to stop 'em about halfway up the slope.'

'They'll be trapped between us and the posse.'

'That's it. And look . . . here they are.'

Ash had no need to point them out. A little cluster of dots was moving in the far distance. Behind these first dots came a bigger crowd of dots. Sam and Ash had an eagle's-eye view of the hunt.

The outlaws had spread into a long line as they wound round the rocks, raising a winding string of dust. Now the nearest dots had grown into men beating their horses to race ever faster in the early morning light. They urged their horses around rocks and over little hills across the rough ground.

Now and then they would turn in their saddles and fire shots, making little puffs of smoke that vanished in a moment. The sun gleamed and glinted on rifle barrels and shiny harness rings.

And the ones behind—the law, the posse led by the sheriff, they raised a big chasing cloud of dust as they too drew nearer.

The outlaws were making for their hole, their little rocky canyon in the mountain-side where they knew they would be safe. Once they were in their hole, they could strike back as a snake from its crack in the rocks.

But the outlaws did not know that their haven was now guarded by their enemies.

'Don't forget,' said Ash, 'we want 'em to go to ground. I want the sheriff to take as many as possible back for trial —we want as few as possible buried here.'

'And we do that by giving 'em a shock.'

'And how. You see that stripey rock there, not far up the slope?'

Sam saw the one—flat on top with yellow streaks down its sides.

'Yeah.'

'Well, when the first rider reaches it, we both fire.'

'I've only got fifteen shots and you've sixteen so . . .'

'Fire ten as fast as you can. Don't aim at the riders, aim

87

at the rock. Twenty slugs in about thirty seconds all hitting at once and screaming off in all directions should make 'em think. They should duck for cover.'

'If they don't?'

'And if they don't, well, we stop the first two. You go for the first one and I'll take the second. If them two go down, then they'll be sure they have no friends up here.'

'Right.'

In an amazingly short time, riders were reaching the bottom of the slope. Sam aimed at the rock. He held his sights on it, ready to fire the moment the first rider passed the rock.

Then they came: the first outlaw urging his weary horse up the beginning of the slope. A bunch of others came close behind him—one of them reeling in his saddle. Others had been left sprawled in the sand, for a couple of riderless horses were following the little crowd.

The black shape passed before Sam's sights, and he began firing his Winchester as fast as he could. He counted as he pumped out the shots and he could see out of the corner of his eye that Ash was doing the same.

A cloud of powder smoke drifted for a moment in front of Sam, then it was whipped away by the morning breeze. The scene lay clear before them.

Sixteen

By this time about half of the outlaws had jumped from their saddles to crouch behind their horses or nearby rocks. Most of them held their pistol or rifle in one hand, and the reins of their horse in the other. Sam could see them searching the cliff with keen eyes for signs of this enemy on their doorstep.

The outlaws still on their horses had stopped, turning their horses in uncertain circles. This was something they could hardly believe was happening. Here they were within gunshot of safety, and somebody began firing in their faces. It was like finding a pack of strange dogs snarling at you from your own bunkhouse door.

'This is neither one thing nor the other,' said Sam, urgently. 'Some are still on their horses. We should get 'em out of their saddles.'

He glanced at Ash, who nodded.

'Right, stop the first man, Sam. Now!'

Sam aimed at the first man: a short figure wearing a bright shirt and a black hat pulled well down over his face. He fired, and heard Ash's shot a second later.

The first man pitched out of his saddle, landing heavily on the ground. The man behind twisted his horse round a rock at the very instant that Ash fired. The shot was close enough to make the man duck his face down on to his horse's head.

The men who were still mounted turned their horses to gallop back, but they were too late. The posse came sweeping over a low rise, making the trap complete.

The man hit by Sam got up, staggered, fell again, and then crawled to the nearest rock. He held his shoulder which was covered with blood far brighter than his shirt.

The two latest shots that Sam and Ash had fired were enough, and more than enough, for those who were still on their horses. They leaped from their saddles and scrambled to the safety of the nearest rocks.

By this time there were six or seven horses running loose. One began trotting down the slope with reins trailing, and the others followed close behind.

Most of the outlaws faced the posse, but one or two

aimed their guns at the cliff face, hoping for a lucky hit on whoever was stopping them getting to safety.

The sheriff had spread his men so that they formed a rough half-circle. Sam saw a couple of the posse collecting the horses to take them behind some high rocks and away from stray bullets. The outlaws' horses were collected with the rest.

It looked as if the sheriff was preparing for a day-long battle if necessary. Firing was going on all the time. Now and then a howl of pain told that someone had been hit. Sam saw one of the sheriff's men being helped—one leg dragging—back to where the horses were.

'We ain't got many bullets left,' said Sam.

'No, so we can't waste any. We've only three or four left in the Winchesters so we better save them for a serious rush. Just keep peppering away with your six-gun for now. They can't get away. They got to give in.'

Sam agreed and looked down at the bandits who now had the high rocks of the mountain on each side of them, the sheriff's posse behind them, and Sam and Ash in front of them.

'This is what we do,' said Ash. 'We use our rifles if any of them try to make a dash up to the cliff—and we stop 'em. The only way they can get in is if we run out of ammo.'

They fired their pistols, keeping the gang's heads down. The posse was firing all the time from the other direction. Smoke drifted over the rocks.

'Lot of lead flying about down there,' said Ash. 'Guess they're bound to break one way or the other soon.'

Seconds later the bandits tried to rush the cliff. With a yell, five or six jumped up from behind their rocks and began running up the slope, firing up at the cliff as they did so. Before Sam or Ash had time to fire their rifles, two of the outlaws fell from shots fired by the posse.

The rest flung themselves down as lead whined round

their heads and screamed off the rocks beside them. There was the crack-crack of the pistols, and the heavier smack of the rifles. Men shouted to each other above the groans of the wounded. Now and then came the distant sound of frightened horses.

The sun shone down on the yellow sand and the black rocks—and here and there on the red splashes that soon soaked into the baked ground.

Suddenly it seemed that everyone with a gun had started firing at top speed. It was as though an invisible commander had just ordered *Rapid fire*. Bullets whistled up to smash themselves on the cliff face around Ash and Sam. Lead whined off the hard rock as though angry at not finding a better target.

Ash was ducking down after firing a shot, when Sam felt a sharp pain on the side of his neck. He put up a shocked hand to feel for the pulsing blood, but there was only sweat. He had been hit only by a piece of rock chipped off by a bullet.

He looked back over the scene. Some of the posse were now getting so eager, that they were standing up from behind their rocks to fire at the outlaws.

Sam and Ash aimed and fired again and again until Sam shouted: 'I'm out of shells.'

Ash tossed a few over to him.

'Nearly all gone now. Make 'em tell!'

Sam began loading them into his six-gun, but it was almost too late to shoot any more. Most of the outlaws were wounded or out of ammunition. The sheriff's men were closing in, moving from rock to rock as they came in for the kill.

Then it was over. An arm rose above a rock which sheltered many of the outlaws. The hand held a bandanna which it waved to and fro: a red bandanna for a white flag.

The firing faltered and then died away. A man rose to

91

his feet with his arms raised and the bandanna still fluttering from his hand. There was silence, broken only by the cries of a wounded man behind a rock. The sheriff stood clear of his cover, his rifle was ready and his badge glittered in the morning sunshine.

'Throw down your guns, put your hands up and come out from the rocks.'

Another bandit stood up and threw down his gun, then another and another. Soon all the unwounded outlaws were standing clear of the rocks with their hands raised.

The men of the posse got up and climbed over rocks and walked towards the bandits, their eyes as ready as their guns for the first sign of treachery. Two or three men began collecting guns while others came with ropes to tie the hands of the prisoners.

One of the sheriff's men ran on in front of the others to the entrance to the canyon. Sam could not mistake the angle of the pipe, even at that distance.

'Let's go down and see Charley,' said Ash. 'He'll be wondering if we made it all right.'

They scrambled down the rocks carrying their Winchesters, and with their six-guns stuck in their belts. The sheriff and Charley were looking over the two sentries who were still lying tied along with Fatty. They all looked up when Sam and Ash came over the rocks.

'I guessed it must have been you two up there,' said the sheriff. 'Score is three wounded on our side and seven wounded and one dead on theirs. We seem to have got most of them, but the older Foley brother is missing. It looks like he's got away somehow. Still ...'

'Mart Foley?' said Ash. 'I'd forgotten about him. We got him for you, sheriff, as well as this fat one here. He was brought in to do all their driving for 'em. Oh, and there's another ...'

'Where you got Foley?'

'Well, you see, sheriff, we came across him early in the night in the stable, so we had to hide him somewhere.'

'We had to hide him and the gold,' said Sam.

'It seemed that the only way to get all the gang out of the canyon was to make them believe that Mart Foley had run off with all the loot. So we had to find a hiding place in the canyon.'

Two of the deputies had joined them by this time.

'We knew the whole place would be searched for Foley and the gold,' said Ash, as he led the way towards the shacks. 'They'd search the mine openings and behind likely rocks. So the only place that might be missed is in here.'

They had arrived at the bunkhouse door which Ash swung open. They crowded in, looking at the bunks that lined the walls from floor to ceiling. Ash went to one of the darkest corners and then turned to the deputies.

'Up there,' he said.

The two men climbed to the topmost bunk. They pulled away old rags and sacks, and there beneath them, gagged and tied firmly to the bunk, was Mart Foley. The deputies untied him and dragged him none too gently to the floor.

One said: 'Them old bed-bugs sure had a feed on him.'

'Phew! He smells of old sacks,' said the other. 'Let's get him out in the open air.'

They freed the other outlaw, the drunken sentry, who was tied down to a bunk in another corner. As they got outside, the other Foley brother was being brought in. Rab Foley looked and walked like a defeated man. His right shirt sleeve was ripped to the shoulder. His bandanna, stained a bright red, was wound round and round his fore-arm. The brothers looked at each other, but said nothing.

'The way I figure it,' said the sheriff, 'is that somehow you managed to get Rab Foley here to think that his brother had gone off with the coach and the gold, but all the time he was hidden here. What I don't understand, is what you did with the coach.'

Sam grinned, but before he could say anything, Mart Foley broke his silence.

'That ain't difficult to figure,' he sneered. 'If they searched the whole place and it ain't there, then ...'

'Then what?'

'Then they burnt it, that's what. While they were all in the shack drinking, these two got the coach to the end of the canyon and burnt it. Too dark to see the ashes—that's why it wasn't seen later.'

'And the gold?'

'Buried it—that's easy done.'

Sam laughed and Ash said:

'Bring 'em along, they'll like watching this.'

They went to the stable.

'Get some harness for the Fargo horses.'

A few minutes later they had fitted the harness on the horses in the pole corral near the pool and Ash led them out. Sam went on in front and began searching the sandy soil and rock rubble by the pool.

'Here it is,' he called out, as Ash came with the lead horse. He held up the end of a heavy chain. Ash backed the horses until the end of the chain could be looped round and fastened to the harness.

'All right, steady as you go.'

'Right—Hup, hup!'

The horses took the strain on the chain which led down over the sloping ground down into the pool itself.

'Hup—hup!'

The horses moved steadily forward as more and more of the chain appeared. A moment later, the roof of the coach broke the surface.

Out of the water and the early-morning shadows came the coach. Shining-wet, streaming, splashing—spilling

94

water down its painted sides with every step the horses made, it came jerking and swaying out of the black water like a hungry monster. The iron-rimmed wheels crushed tracks in the pebbly sand until it stopped on dry land once more. Still the water dripped like pale blood from a dozen wounds, and strands of green weedy hair clung to its roof.

The Foley brothers stared with regretful eyes as they thought of the gold they had lost—gold they had exchanged for long weary years in jail, if they managed to escape the hangman's necktie.

'Take 'em away,' said the sheriff.

Sam went to look at the coach.

'All that water's ruined the seats,' he said, 'but I guess the Company ain't gonna quibble about that.'

'How'd you get it in there?' asked the sheriff.

'Went in a lot easier than it came out,' said Sam. 'Me and Ash here just took the brake off and pushed just a little at a time to keep it quiet. Then on this slope here it went in as though it was dying of thirst.'

The sheriff climbed on the coach to have a look at the chest.

'Well, come on, Sam,' said Ash, 'the sheriff will square all this up and see the coach is driven to Bear Cross.'

'We got to get our horses,' said Sam, thinking of Straw's long wait for him.

'No need to, here they are.'

Sam looked round and there was Charley leading Ash's pinto and Straw. Charley waggled his pipe at them as he spoke without taking it out of his mouth.

'Thought you'd like to be off and running, so I picked up your horses for you.'

'We'd sure like to be moving,' said Sam. 'I've seen all I want to of this place. What I'd like now is a double helping of chicken and hot rice, and then sleep for a coupla days.'

He swung himself up on Straw's back.

95

'See you sometime,' called out the sheriff as he walked away, then he turned back. 'Oh, Ash, I nearly forgot to tell you. It came over the wire that they want you at Crystal Lake. They're having trouble with the stage line there. You'll see the message in the office.'

Sam and Ash rode off in single file, while Charley just sat on his horse and watched them go. They rode past the stable, the shacks, and then out through the corridor of rock.

'Sam?' said Ash, as they rode side by side down the wide slope.

'Yeah?'

'What do you think about Crystal Lake? I'd like to have you along.'

'Crystal Lake! You know, Ash, there was one place I was always thinking of visiting . . .'

'Crystal Lake?'

'No, it was San Francisco, but maybe that will be the way I'll go—through Crystal Lake.' Sam reached forward and patted Straw on her neck. 'What do you think, Straw?'

But Straw didn't care where she went.

Ash reined in his horse when they got to the bottom of the slope and turned to look back. Sam stopped by his side. They stared up at the towering cliffs of the mountainside.

'You know something, Sam, when you look at it from here, it's hard to believe there's a canyon back there. Nowhere's a good name for it, 'cause at the end of today when everybody's left, it'll be nowhere again.'

'Lost and gone—maybe for good this time.'

'Yeah, it's unlikely there'll ever be another stage to Nowhere. Well, come on, Sam, first stop Bear Cross and then tomorrow we'll head for Crystal Lake.'